PARISH AND EMPIRE

# Parish and Empire

## STUDIES AND SKETCHES

*by*
JACK SIMMONS

COLLINS
ST JAMES'S PLACE, LONDON
1952

PRINTED IN GREAT BRITAIN
COLLINS CLEAR-TYPE PRESS : LONDON AND GLASGOW

# CONTENTS

# ILLUSTRATIONS

## MAPS

# PREFACE

THESE ESSAYS vary widely in subject; but all of them are intended to illustrate certain main themes, which run through the whole book. Those themes are stated in the opening study, "Local, National, and Imperial History". Although this originated as an inaugural lecture, I make no apology for including it here, since it was designed at the time of its delivery to set out a programme of work, of which this book is an early instalment.

I believe, as I have tried to make plain there, that the integration of our local history with that of Britain and the British Empire offers a great opportunity to students of history in our time. I am not suggesting, of course, that no work of this kind has been done in the past: that would be to ignore such books as Freeman's *English Towns and Districts* and Maitland's *Domesday Book and Beyond*, to name only two classics. But the task is more pressing for us than it has ever been before. The *Victoria County History* already runs to nearly a hundred volumes, the *Transactions* and *Proceedings* of the main county societies to many more than a thousand. The material they contain is being absorbed into our national history only very slowly. I believe the pace could be, and ought to be, quickened; and the process should, I think, be extended in some new directions. Two are suggested in this book. The history of English transport can be satisfactorily written only if its local and national aspects are considered side by side, in the closest relation with each other. And I think there is much to be learnt about British imperial trade and settlement from a study of the local affiliations, back in England, of the traders and settlers, as Professor Hattersley has recently shown us in *The British Settlement of Natal*. What volumes of imperial history, too, are waiting to be written from the monuments in English country churches !

This book does not attempt to bring all these topics into scale with one another. It is no more than what its sub-title proclaims : a set of " Studies and Sketches", designed to show something of the diversity of subjects that is before us and the range of material that is available for their illustration. It is also intended to display what I believe to be the importance of the visual study of history —again, no new idea, but one that can, in my view, be pursued much further and more thoroughly than it has been in the past.

These themes will receive fuller and more systematic discussion in a new co-operative work, for whose planning and editing I am responsible : a " Survey of England," the first volumes of which will be published by Messrs. Collins before very long. The English counties, and about a dozen of the most important English towns, will each be treated in a separate volume by a single author. It will be among the chief objects of the Survey to incorporate and re-interpret the bulky local evidence, and to explain the relationship that the county or town bears to England as a whole, the part it has played and is playing now in our national life.

These essays, then, are preliminary to further work that is to come. But they are quite independent, and I should like them to be read on their own, in and for themselves. Some of them have been published before, though usually in a somewhat different form : others are printed here for the first time. For permission to reproduce essays the copyright of which I do not control I am obliged to the Council of University College, Leicester, the Committee of the Leicestershire Archæological Society, and the editors of the *Spectator*, *Time and Tide*, *Devon and Cornwall Notes and Queries*, and the *West Country Magazine*.

For help in some points of research and in the finding of illustrations I am grateful to the County Archivist of Essex, Mr. F. G. Emmison, and his Senior Assistant, Miss Hilda Grieve; to Dr. C. H. Thompson—now County Archivist of Surrey, formerly of Leicestershire; to Mr. John A. Chatterton, Clerk to the Leicestershire County Council, and to Mrs. Griffin, of the County Rooms, Leicester; to Mr. W. A. Seaby, Keeper of Taunton Castle Museum, and his Assistant Keeper, Mr. A. D. Hallam; to Mr. H. St. George Gray and Mr. T. D. Tremlett. My thanks are also due to the Director of the National Buildings Record for permission to reproduce the illustration of the roof of Chelmsford Cathedral facing page 129.

Finally, I must acknowledge the great kindness of four friends who have done much for the book. Mr. A. L. Rowse first suggested that I should bring these essays together. Any one who is acquainted with his work—and especially with those two great studies, *Tudor Cornwall* and *The England of Elizabeth*—will see how very much I owe to his example. Mr. Michael Robbins read the book in proof, and it has benefited greatly from his astringent and constructive comments. Capt. L. H. Irvine prepared the index, with his usual meticulous care. Mr. Norman Scarfe criticised and forced me to improve the book at every stage in its production : it owes a great deal of what merits it may now possess to his steady and kind assistance.

J. S.

*University College, Leicester*
12 *August* 1951

# LOCAL, NATIONAL, AND IMPERIAL
# HISTORY

THE PAST few years have seen a striking development in
the study of English local history. Until quite lately it
was generally considered a field of minor importance :
valuable, no doubt, in its way, but essentially an affair of
the parish pump, the business of antiquaries, not historians.
Now we are beginning to think differently, to recognise
that local history, if its study is pursued in an intelligent
and critical spirit, may be regarded as a branch of the
history of England as a whole, comparable in importance,
for example, with ecclesiastical or military history, having
its own materials, its own technique, its own discipline.
I wish here to discuss briefly the relationship it bears to
the national history of England and then to extend the
horizon further, to the history of the British Empire
beyond.[1]

I have placed these three branches of history in this
order not as an order of importance, ascending or descending, but simply for convenience of treatment. It seems to
me natural to begin with local history, the history of what
we all know best and most intimately. I shall draw my
examples from all parts of the country—from the East
Midlands several times, but also from the West and the
North.

[1] This is a slightly amended version of an Inaugural Lecture delivered at
University College, Leicester, on 16 February 1948.

Let me begin with a Leicestershire illustration.

Not long ago I made my way out eastwards, one Saturday afternoon, from Leicester to Tilton, where the Digby family once lived. There is a monument of one of them in the church : Everard Digby, who died in 1509. As you look at the figure on the tomb, you get a strange sense of the continuity of history. For that man's father was killed as a Lancastrian at the battle of Towton ; his great-great-grandson, of the same names, was a leading conspirator in the Gunpowder Plot ; and the conspirator's eldest son, Sir Kenelm Digby, was one of the richest, most famous, fantastic, and wayward personalities of the seventeenth century.

It was a cold November day, the wind whistling round the top of the exposed hill on which Tilton stands : even the sunlight seemed somehow chilly as I walked south-wards by the up-and-down bridle road to Skeffington. Here I had one purpose : to see if any trace remained of the great member of the Skeffington family—Sir William, Lord Deputy of Ireland under Henry VIII, who married, incidentally, the sister of that Everard Digby who lies in Tilton church. Sir William died in Dublin and is buried in St. Patrick's. At Skeffington a monument was erected to his memory ; but, as Nichols tells us in his *History of Leicestershire*, it was " demolished by the impiety of the last age "—in other words, like so much else, it perished in the Civil War. Still, the big house remains, perhaps built by him, close to the church.

And then, as the afternoon wore on, I walked back along the main road to Billesdon. There I wanted to see the grammar school, which has had, in the course of its long history, one very distinguished pupil, and perhaps two. It is certain that young George Villiers was sent to school there, until he was taken away by his mother in 1606 ;

and a bare ten years later, when he had risen through the favour of James I and become Earl of Buckingham, we find him remembering Billesdon, securing for the little town the privileges of a market. (I cannot help adding the traditional story, it pleased me so much when I came upon it : that Buckingham was moved in the matter by his old schoolmaster, who hoped that the market would bring more alehouses to Billesdon and improve the quality of the beer.) Less certainly this school can boast as a pupil another of the great Leicestershire men of the seventeenth century—George Fox, the founder of the Society of Friends ; though I am afraid it cannot claim to have taught him very much, if one is to judge by the spelling of his *Journal*. Unluckily, the original building has disappeared. The school was rebuilt—no doubt near its old site—in 1640. There it stands on the east side of the churchyard, a modest, decent, square stone building. It reminds you of the little school below the church at Hawkshead in Lancashire, where Wordsworth was educated ; and the other, so like it, at Grantham, of which Isaac Newton was once head boy. They are all three types of those old grammar schools that have contributed so much to the making of England.

Here was only a short afternoon's walk—not more than five miles all told : yet what worlds of history it opened up ! I have chosen it as an illustration of the close link between our local and national life. The two are inextricably bound up together. Perhaps that truth seems obvious enough. But it is often forgotten ; and in one way, perhaps, more than any other. The history of England has generally been written in terms of the history of London : the part played by the provinces, the difference between their outlook and London's, have frequently been ignored.    London has been our capital for so many centuries, our greatest city, and for such a long time the greatest city in the world, that its predominance in England is quite beyond challenge. But it remains true, nevertheless, that London is not England; and true also, I think, that much of our history has been written as if London *were* England. If we wish to understand English history, it is not enough to watch Council and Parliament at Westminster, to attend to the activities of London merchants, the building-up of the City, or to consider the literature and the art of London alone. To understand it aright, we must go out into the provinces also.

Perhaps I may make this point clearer by two examples : one taken from political history, the other from the history of our art. From the sixteenth century to the nineteenth, English political life was dominated by what may broadly be called one governing class. The centre of politics was always London ; but most of the politicians came from the provinces, where their social and economic position was founded. We shall not understand these men, or the part they played in English government, unless we examine their life at home, the way they made their money, their relations with their neighbours. For many political combinations have been reared and broken by such alliances and quarrels : think of the age-long feud between the Greys and the Hastings in Leicestershire, and all its consequences. And in the eighteenth century, as Professor Namier has shown us, the closest study of these local affiliations is necessary for a full understanding of the structure of British politics.

Or again, consider the history of English art. In the earlier Middle Ages I think it would be true to say that the centre of artistic creation is seldom to be found in London. In the fourteenth and fifteenth centuries it was at Nottingham that the delicate alabaster work of England was made, much of it to be exported to France and Spain. Move forward three hundred years and look at our architecture. The greatest men, beyond doubt, worked in London; but it would be a most incomplete survey that omitted to consider the two Woods and the minor masters like the Smiths of Warwick and Carr of York. The same thing is true of painting. The Norwich School springs to one's mind, and here again there are lesser provincial artists, working by themselves but making, none the less, their own small and definite contribution— Barker of Bath, Brown of Shrewsbury, William Turner of Oxford.

I do not wish to labour my point any further. I would rather pass on to the general contention of which these are only particular examples. A true understanding of England's past can be attained only by studying local and national history side by side. It is clearly not useful to embark on a study of local history wholly by itself, with the county or town or village one is examining for one's widest horizon: to study the history of the Leicestershire coal-field—shall we say?—without a thorough grounding in the technical and economic development of English coal-mining as a whole. But the converse is also true. History is primarily the study of past life, and if we limit our study to the nation as a whole we lose some touch with life: we miss, above all, the variety, the rich differences that are to be found all through life, are part of life itself. If some of those who have tried to impose patterns and formulae upon history had studied local history in all its meaning in their own countries, I cannot help thinking they would have ended by putting their formulae into the fire.

Now it is here, I believe, that a small University College can make a distinctive contribution to historical studies.

One of the greatest problems that confronts us today—
and I suppose it is the same in all fields of learning—is the
problem of specialisation. The work of our predecessors
accumulates relentlessly, volume by volume, until it fills
large libraries. Two hundred years ago it was still possible
for one historian to master all the sources of information
that were available to him ; to write his narrative, incorporating in it all the facts and ideas that seemed to him
significant ; and at the end of it, to feel that he had achieved
some kind of finality about a great theme—the decline and
fall of the Roman Empire, for instance. Today that is
quite out of the question. The mass of evidence, discovered
and discoverable, is far too large. The historian is therefore
forced to confine himself to narrower and narrower topics.
If he is writing, for example, on English history, he cannot
hope to add anything valuable to our knowledge unless he
restricts himself to a small corner of that great field : a
short period of time, or a single aspect—Parliament, it
may be, or the Church, or overseas trade. In doing so he
must miss the sweep and range of the older historians, the
sense of looking at the development of a people as a whole
over a long span of years. The danger is clear. His view
is microscopic : it quickly becomes myopic too.

The study of local history can offer something important
towards a solution of this problem. For it is still possible
to examine the history of a town or a county or even a
whole region of England over a long period, to illustrate
and test out there the generalisations that national historians
have made. It is possible to do this because the scale is
still small, and the literature of the subject not unmanage-
able. How profitable it is may be seen from Mr. Rowse's
book *Tudor Cornwall*, which, though it is confined to the
study of a single county, yet has more to teach us about
the life of the sixteenth century than most of the standard

works on the history of Tudor England.  For Mr. Rowse
is able in that book to draw what he calls the " portrait
of a society ", and he looks at that society as a whole,
describing it with a minute exactitude that would be
unattainable nowadays by any historian who was writing
about England on a national scale.  And it is that very
minuteness, the detail, that makes his portrait live for us.

There is a great deal of room for the wider application
of these methods, for their extension to other types of
society ; and surely this development could come most
appropriately from the civic Universities and University
Colleges.  Might it not be one of their aims to carry further
such intensive inquiry into the history of the English
provinces ?  So many profitable lines of development lie
ahead.  Not a single one of the great English towns has a
large-scale history worthy of its past.  What inadequate
attention has so far been paid to the local history of nineteenth-century politics, and how much is wanting, for that
very reason, to our knowledge and understanding of the
Victorian age !  Or again, to take another instance, we
know far too little about the history of our county families
—those Digbys and Skeffingtons and Hastings and Greys
I was referring to just now.  True, their genealogies
have been investigated.  There they lie, stretched out over
the pages of Nichols and the *Complete Peerage*.  But that is
only the beginning of the task.  We need some one to
come and put life into those bare family trees, to tell us
just who all these men were, what dowries they got with
their wives, how they bought and sold at the Dissolution
of the Monasteries and in the Civil War, what they invested
their money in under the Georges and how they voted
(the two things may, or may not, be linked together), what
difference the development of industry made to them, how
they fared in the Agricultural Depression—yes, and how

they are faring now in the social revolution of the twentieth
century. Family history of that kind, steadily pursued, will
constantly throw new light on English politics : without
it there is no possibility whatever of a true understanding
of the development of English society.

There are many important topics in economic history
that demand similar illustration, at once from a local and
a national point of view. English transport provides a
good example. Perhaps I may refer to one branch of it
in which I am particularly interested myself : the development of railways. It is remarkable that scarcely any serious
academic study of that subject has yet been attempted in
this country—the greatest work that we have yet had on
the general history of our railways was written by a German
some seventy years ago. Yet this is a field of exceptional
interest and importance, for it was in Britain that each of
the crucial advances in the technique and administration
of railways down to 1850 took place. Britain, in fact, may
fairly claim to be the inventor of the modern railway—and
claims of that kind can rarely be put forward, for techno-
logical development usually bears an international character.

The subject needs investigating at many different
points : by engineers, statisticians, commercial lawyers.
But again, too much attention must not be concentrated
on London, on parliamentary legislation, the policy laid
down by government. Often—much too often—no policy
was laid down by government. It is only by studying the
history of the separate companies that one can reach the
heart of the matter. They developed untidily, each in close
rivalry with its neighbours, some slower, some quicker,
according to wealth, opportunity, incentive, accident.
Each of them retained some peculiar features, which make
many generalisations about their history doubtful or false.
Even today you can discern those differences if you look

for them, and they will never be wholly obliterated by nationalisation.

Now the basis of this study must, in the first place, be local : the local press ; local documents of all kinds, deeds, conveyances, letters ; the railways themselves, their physical structure and buildings. It is only in conjunction with such work as this that one can profitably use the material collected in London—Parliamentary Papers and so on—and the documents available there, at the Public Record Office, in the archives of the British Transport Commission.

I have been speaking so far mainly of research, of books that have been written in the past and may be written in the future. Let us turn now to look at the other side of university work, the teaching side. What can this combined study of local and national history offer here ? In a sentence, my answer is this : I believe it can offer the best and straightest introduction possible to a great many historical problems of high importance.

Broadly speaking, our knowledge of history is based on two kinds of evidence : on words, written and spoken ; and on the actual relics of the past that have survived for us. The first class depends, obviously, on books ; but the second is quite different. This is evidence that has to be seen and touched and handled. There are branches of history in which both sorts of evidence have always been used together. Archaeology, for example. It is plainly impossible to learn archaeology from books alone. No book can be a substitute for the use of the spade, the investigation of the site ; the archaeologist will often derive more from knowing exactly where and how an object was found than from a study of the object itself—and incomparably more, it goes without saying, than from a mere photograph of the object or a description in the text

of a book. But the same is true of the study of modern
history also. Here too one must see the things one is
reading about. And indeed they lie all around us. Look
at Leicester. What other town is there in England that
can show a sight just like that which appears as your
train draws into the Central station? The castle across
the river, its Norman hall encased in nineteenth-century
brick; St. Mary de Castro, a most remarkable church;
the spire of the cathedral in the distance—one of the
triumphs of Victorian architecture, a study in noble proportion; then, close to you, St. Nicholas', with its Saxon
nave and delightful Norman tower; in front of it the
Roman forum; and, as if that were not enough, a Roman
pavement actually lies underneath as you step out on to
the station platform. I shall never forget my excitement
when I first saw Leicester from the train. It is a scene
that I put beside others, more famous and beautiful but
hardly more remarkable: Dover from the sea, the terraces
of Bath, Lincoln in the distance on its hill.

For here are the visible, the tangible memorials of the
past. And to study history in books only is deliberately
to reject a great body of historical evidence. A student of
history should spend much of his time out in the field. If
he does not, he will never get into close touch with the
life of the people he is studying. His work, whatever pains
he may take, will be two-dimensional: he will not see his
subject in the round. At Leicester, for instance, the student
should see something of the city itself, and of the East
Midlands at his door: the villages and farmhouses, at
their most beautiful in the stone-belt; the historic towns
—Nottingham, the greatest; Derby, with its splendid
Gibbs cathedral; Stamford, where time seems almost
to have been suspended since 1750. And everywhere the
churches: not only their fabrics, but their fittings, which

illustrate the variety and excellence of English craftsman-
ship ; and their monuments, whose inscriptions form a
great mass of historical material that has not yet been used
as it might be.

I firmly believe that this is the right way to study
history, and the right way to teach it too : that both these
kinds of evidence must be used side by side. But there is
a serious practical obstacle in the way of using these
methods as they might, and should, be used. We are not,
as a University College, free to teach as we like. We are
limited at all points by the syllabus of London University ;
and it is a large and very exacting syllabus. I am not concerned at the moment with discussing its merits in general.
The College derives, as I am sure it recognises, very substantial advantages from its connexion with London, from
sending its students in for the London degrees with their
high reputation. But in history the syllabus is based
exclusively on books ; it takes no account of local varia-
tions ; it is concerned predominantly with political history
—a single branch of the subject ; and it lays the heaviest
stress upon fact, to the detriment, in my opinion, of
imaginative interpretation, the subtlest and highest achievement of the student of history. It demands so much time
to get through the mass of reading that is prescribed by
the London syllabus that we are severely limited in the
amount of historical field-work we can undertake. None
the less, we are making a start with a modest programme.

From a consideration of the syllabus we are now working under, it is natural to pass on to think of one we might
look forward to in the future : the syllabus of a Leicester
school of history, when the College has achieved a wholly
independent status. I have already hinted at some of the
features that I think it should include. In the first place
it should, to my mind, be as flexible as possible. It should

offer the widest reasonable range of options, for it is most important to allow the student, as far as it is practicable, to follow the particular bent of his mind. I should favour the introduction of special subjects in local history and provision—which is, of course, made elsewhere—for offering a short thesis, perhaps as a necessary requirement for the award of a first-class degree.

In some other respects I should like to see a school of history developing on rather different lines from those I am acquainted with. I believe the study of history in England has given disproportionate attention to man as an administrator, too little to some aspects of his intellectual and spiritual life, and far too little to his aesthetic achievement. I am anxious therefore that the study of history should be linked very much more closely with the study of literature and the other arts.

In the Oxford history school, which I passed through, no provision whatever was made for the study of literature. There was, it is true, a general paper—something most desirable, by the way, that the London syllabus lacks— and it contained questions on literature, music, and art, as well as on politics and on historical technique. The usual single questions on aesthetic matters were also included in the papers on English and European history; but they were hidden away shyly, apologetically so to speak, in a corner of the paper behind all those formidable questions on the political achievement of Walpole and the economic consequences of the Black Death. It is possible to get a first-class degree at Oxford—and as far as I know this is true of all English universities—without ever having opened the works of Shakespeare, or (still more curious) of Clarendon or Gibbon or Macaulay.

The reason is to be found in the history of the Oxford school of history itself. It grew out of the school of law, from which it was separated only in 1872 ; and the marks of its origin remain strongly upon it. I am certainly not wishing to decry the school. It has made a great contribution not only to the study and teaching of history but to the whole intellectual life of England during the past half-century. My point is that though it is a very fine school I believe that others could profitably be developed on different lines ; and especially that there is something to be said for giving rather less time to the study of institutions and rather more to the study of literature.

It seems to me too that a new history school might well broaden out in another direction : by including optional provision for the study of the history of science. The gravest problem here would be one of teaching, for the subject must be taught by some one with a double training, as historian and as scientist. It is one of those disciplines that occupy a no-man's-land between two others. But we are now beginning to see its emergence as a separate branch of study. Separate, though not wholly independent—it can never be that ; but what fruitful developments it may bring with it ! How many problems there are in common between the scientist and the historian ! And how few opportunities there have hitherto been for a study of them in common ! Does not the development of the history of science offer a means of linking scientific and historical method, or at any rate of bringing them into touch with each other ? And are there not many students whose minds and tastes are adapted to that combined study ?

I suggest, then, that the syllabus of the history school in a small civic university might well provide for the study of some aspect of local history ; of British history as a whole—and by that I do not mean political history only ; of some part of the aesthetic, intellectual, or spiritual

achievement of man. But that is not all. I do not think
the field should be confined to Britain : some effort must
be made to examine a fraction of the history of the outer
world. It can be no more than a fraction—here we are
back again at the problem of the accumulation of evidence.
But there is a real value in projecting one's mind out from
the conditions one is accustomed to in one's own country
into the different environment of Europe or another
continent.

It has been usual—in fact, the practice has been almost
universal—for schools of history in English universities
to insist on some study of European history. There is
very much to be said in favour of this provision. A good
knowledge of the development of Europe is a most important aid to the understanding of the history of England,
and it is indispensable to the study of English civilisation.
Yet I am uncertain, in my own mind, if it should be made
compulsory. I believe that some part, at any rate, of the
history of British expansion overseas might be a desirable
alternative. If I pass on now to the third division of my
subject, imperial history, it is not because I wish to slight
the study of the history of Europe—I believe that for some
students it is the most valuable part of their training ; but
because I wish to develop the claims of imperial history
upon us, which have been much less widely recognised.

The scientific study of the history of the British Empire
is scarcely more than fifty years old. It begins pretty
definitely with two works published close together :
Egerton's *Short History of British Colonial Policy*, dating
from 1897, and Sir William Hunter's *History of British India*
—which remains, alas, a fragment through the death of
its author, when only two volumes had appeared, in 1900.
In 1905 the first chair of colonial history in a British
university was established, at Oxford, and Egerton was

appointed to it. Since then three other similar chairs have been set up, at London, Cambridge, and Bristol; and the subject has made its way slowly and timidly into the curricula of most of our universities.

The study is thus of very recent origin. And it has all the freshness of new work. The first generation of imperial historians concentrated their attention mainly on the constitutional aspects of the British Empire, and almost exclusively on the Dominions and India. Work on its economic history started later—it was originated by the American historian G. L. Beer, and Americans have continued to take a leading part in it ever since. It is only in the last twenty years that any serious investigation has begun of the history of the dependent Empire in tropical Africa and South-East Asia. The pioneer there has been Sir Reginald Coupland, under whom I am very proud to have worked at Oxford. He has broken entirely new ground with his two large volumes on the history of East Africa, besides giving us the most important study we have yet had of the political system of British India.

It is now, in work such as this, that we are just beginning to examine this huge field of historical inquiry. It seems to me an interesting field for several different reasons. The study of imperial history, especially in Africa and the East, brings us face to face with one of the greatest problems of the modern world : that of the contact between different peoples at varying stages of civilisation. What is called the opening-up of Africa has been in progress for little more than a century and a half : it is still in progress today. Here the modern historian may attempt to join present to past (and that is one of the most difficult tasks an historian can attempt), to describe a great human movement not as finished, complete, but as something that is still happening before his eyes. It is a striking opportunity : a field that has been little worked and offers big rewards. Its successful cultivation will demand a rather new technique, in which the historian must learn a great deal from the sociologist, the anthropologist, and the colonial administrator.

To the student of politics the history of the British Commonwealth offers material of extraordinary interest, in the adaptation of British institutions to the differing needs of the Dominions, of India and the tropical Empire. It has not always been a successful process : there have been failures, serious mistakes—I am thinking at the moment of the history of Ceylon. On the other side there are great positive achievements to show : the working of the federal constitution of Canada is, I think, one ; the development of social security in New Zealand, from its tentative beginnings, another. More often, as in all human politics, the success and the failure have been mixed. But the value of such studies as these is obvious ; for we are still confronted by problems of the same kind, and we ourselves are responsible for their solution.

Here is a third reason why I think imperial history can be read with so much more profit and interest. It is the record of the impact of Britain upon the world beyond Europe. And hence it seems to me that imperial history can properly take its place as an undergraduate study on a level with European history. For it is not to be considered a narrower field. True, it does not demand a knowledge of foreign languages—as European history, if it is to be read with intelligent understanding, undoubtedly does : yet, on the other hand, imperial history is concerned with societies much more remote from us, in spirit as in space, than France or the Netherlands or Germany. And at every point it grows out of the history of Britain itself. It is dominated by the history and ideas of Englishmen— the people whose minds we can most readily understand.

That brings me to the thing that interests me most of all in the history of the British Empire : the lives of the men who made it. I do not mean only, or even primarily, the great. I am thinking of the lives of lesser men, the men upon whom the main work of building up the British administration has rested. So often, going about England, you come upon a tablet in a church that commemorates one of them—in St. Mary's at Nottingham a long account of a young man who spent all his life in the navy, serving in the squadron for the suppression of the slave trade in West Africa, until he died on that pestilent station in his early twenties ; at Taunton another youngster, who died in 1829, as the inscription simply records, " at Pondigul, East Indies, far from any European station ". He may stand for tens of thousands of others. How well those bare words hint at the desperate loneliness of their life up country, in jungle or bush, their isolation in the midst of an alien world !

Or again, the missionaries. What strange, remarkable men they were ! Livingstone, beyond question the greatest ; Robert Moffat, his father-in-law ; Roger Williams and Selwyn and Patteson, who have left their mark plainly on New Zealand and the Pacific to this day ; William Carey, who went out from his chapel in Leicester to lay the foundations of Christianity in Bengal. It is difficult for us, living in the world of twentieth-century rationalism, to penetrate the minds of missionaries, whether they are Jesuits in Japan or Victorian Scots in Africa. Nothing easier than to dismiss them out of hand, to ferret out whatever can be said to their disgrace or their ridicule, and to pass on, leaving their effort as something irrelevant on one side. But that is to ignore something very important —and for the worst of all possible reasons, because we find it difficult to understand and explain. I suggest that the whole history of Christian missions, and their part in the development of modern imperialism, needs to be investigated : not by some one who is concerned to decry or score off them (that will get us nowhere), nor on the other hand by a tame apologist, whose history will quickly become hagiology, but by a sensible, sympathetic observer with an open mind. There can be no doubt of the importance of the subject. The whole development of education in the colonies, to take one example out of many, has been profoundly influenced—it has often been dominated—by the missionaries.

We have never, I think, taken adequate notice of the effect of this export of so many men of high ability and character upon the development of Britain itself. In a way, that is quite natural. We have such a long history as an imperial power that we have come to take it for granted. The Victorians assumed without question, even without remark, that a quota of the very ablest young men in the country would go out each year to give the best of their lives to service in India. It was not until the eighties and nineties that Englishmen at home began to be widely aware of the work their countrymen were doing in the East, and then it was from Kipling, the detached, almost foreign observer, and from Conrad, the Pole, that they learnt of it. Looking back now, at a moment when the British Empire is shrinking, we can see all this better than they could. We have heard a great deal about the profits and losses of imperialism—but chiefly about the profits, from British Liberal economists and their Russian and American disciples. Here is a striking item to be set on the side of loss : not something material, which can be reckoned up in terms of cash, but a loss that made Britain substantially poorer in talent all the same. I am far from deploring this fact : far too from suggesting that these men worked without reward, to themselves or the country that exported them.    And I do not wish to overrate their ability.    There were stupid men and nincompoops among them—you remember how Mr. Belloc's Lord Lundy, when he had failed at everything else, received the terrible command, " Go out and govern New South Wales ".    But on the whole the work of these men—from the greatest of them, like Warren Hastings and Elgin, down to thousands whose very names are lost, settlers and traders, engineers and civil servants and soldiers—their work has been done well : it has lasted, and, if a student of history may be allowed to look forward into the future, I think it will be remembered and imitated for many years to come.

We have travelled a long way now, from the uplands of East Leicestershire to Bechuanaland and India and the Pacific.    I have done no more than touch on the fringes of a great subject.    I have tried to indicate where my own interests lie, and some of the ways in which I think history may profitably be studied.    But there is one other question I should like to refer to very briefly—an obvious question enough : why should one study history at all ?    There are indeed many possible answers to that question : let me suggest two.

In the first place, I believe history has a practical value, and that a very high one.    It has a great deal to teach us about our own world.    It can never be an infallible guide, a multiplication table, for human situations never repeat themselves exactly.    But short of that, history does offer an immense, an inexhaustible supply of past experience for us to make use of : without it I believe our politics and economics—to say nothing of other things—will be shallow and often meaningless.

And beside this practical reason for studying history I should like to put another—something more personal :

the pleasure, I almost said the beauty, of the study itself.
This is a feeling common, I think, to most students of
history, though it takes many different forms. The great
historians of the past all knew it. They studied and wrote
history for one reason : because they must. You have
only to read Sir George Trevelyan's *Life and Letters of
Macaulay*—surely one of the most delightful of English
biographies—to see that. Page after page the inimitable
letters go on, filled with the study of history and the joy
that Macaulay took in it. Indeed with him it could scarcely
be called a study at all : it soon became as much a part of
his daily life as eating and drinking. His mind became
possessed by the past. Yet that did not mean that he lost
interest in the present. Very far from it. Few men have
ever lived with greater gusto and vigour. He was in
Parliament for a third of his life, an extremely important
member of the Government of India for four years, then
a cabinet minister at home. But Macaulay's historical work
only deepened and enlarged his study of politics—just as
politics, his experience of government from the inside,
added authority and substance to the *History of England*.

That is speaking of a great man indeed. But any true
student of history will understand and recognise Macaulay's
feeling, his happy absorption in the past, until—though he
remained a politician to his finger-tips—he turned away
from politics, preferring to write history instead. In our
own time Macaulay's successor has been his great-nephew,
Dr. G. M. Trevelyan, and he has defined what is, I think,
the ultimate appeal of history to many of its students.
" Truth ", he says, " is the criterion of historical study ;
but its impelling motive is poetic. Its poetry consists in
its being true." It would hardly be possible to improve on
that statement. Here is what is so affecting about the
relics of the past that remain to us—the very fact that these

things were made by men who are now dead, whom we can never know : whether it is the White Horse on the Downs in Berkshire, or the great church at Melton Mowbray, or a letter, it may be, written during the Civil War. For the moment, as you look at them, time stands still : they have taken on the same reality as the world of today. You have moved back into the past—or rather, past and present have become one.

WE KNOW a great deal about the life of Somerset under the Georges. The literature of the subject, to begin with, is unusually good. We have two contemporary histories of the county to go upon, several most interesting diaries, some first-class letters, at least one little Somerset auto-biography ; and, in addition to all these, modern writers have given us a series of parish histories that most other counties must envy. But we do not need to depend solely on books. So many visible records of that age remain— houses and streets and public buildings, a good deal of the very landscape itself.

In this essay I shall be primarily concerned with rural Somerset. I shall leave out of account the city of Bath, which is a whole world, a subject for a dozen essays on its own. Nor shall I say anything of Bristol, whose administrative independence of Somerset had been established long before.

The period I have chosen, from 1714 to 1830, has some unity of its own, if you do not interpret the opening and closing dates too exactly. In politics it begins with the firm establishment of the Hanoverians on the throne, the reign of the Whig oligarchy. It sees four great wars with France. In the course of the last of them—the Revolutionary and Napoleonic war—the Tories build up an iron ascendancy, which collapses only in 1827 ; and

The Blue-Coat School and Almshouses, Frome

From a drawing by J. Buckler (1845) in the collection of the
Somersetshire Archaeological Society at Taunton Castle

ALTAR-PIECE, MARTOCK CHURCH

From an engraving by T. Bonnor in Collinson's
*History of Somerset* (1791)

the period ends with the struggle over the great Reform Bill in 1832. Echoes of all these events in high politics are to be heard in the quieter, distant world of Somerset.

But this period can be seen in different terms too, and perhaps more vividly. When it began, Defoe was still journeying round the country, taking the notes that he afterwards worked up into his *Tour through the whole Island of Great Britain* : at its end, in the very year of George IV's death, Cobbett published his *Rural Rides*. Or look at it another way. In 1714 the stage-coach was something strange and rare, dragged laboriously over terrible roads : the ordinary way to travel—if you had to, and few people did travel any distance—was on horseback. As the century went on, the roads were improved beyond recognition, coaching became an art (even a pleasure); and then, in 1830, the railway triumphed. All these changes can be watched, too, in Somerset, as they succeed each other one by one.

The first question one naturally asks is : how did Georgian Somerset stand in relation to the other counties of England, what was its population? On the first page of his *History of Somersetshire*, which was written in the 1830s, the Rev. Mr. Phelps was able to point out, perhaps with a touch of comfortable pride, that Somerset ranked seventh in area and eighth in population among the counties of England. Today it remains seventh in area, but it has dropped to the twenty-second place in population.

The main cause of this change in the relative importance of Somerset is clear enough : the growth of the great industrial regions of the Midlands and the North, and the continued expansion of London, while Somerset has remained primarily an agricultural county. In the period I am speaking of, Somerset was itself an important industrial region. In the eighteenth century it was linked with its neighbours, Gloucestershire, Wiltshire, and Devon, to form one of the two great cloth-manufacturing districts of England—until, towards the end of the century, the industry migrated northwards to Yorkshire. Again, the Somerset coal-field was then of much greater relative importance than it is now, when measured against the total production of coal for the whole country.

At the census of 1831, the population of the county was just over 400,000. Thirty years before, it had been 274,000. Before that we can only guess, for the census of 1801 was the first to be taken. From the indications we have, however, it is quite safe to say that the population of Somerset rose during the eighteenth century. As for the towns, it has been calculated, with fair probability, that the population of Taunton about 1700 was a little under 4,000, and we know it was 5,800 in 1801. Frome was at the end of a long period of prosperity about 1790 : from an unofficial census taken then, it appears to have contained 8,100 people.[1] Bath, a mushroom growth of the eighteenth century, had already become much the largest town in the county. By 1831 Bath had some 38,000 people, Frome 12,000, and Taunton 11,000.

Although, as I have said, the industries of Somerset were very important, the foundation of the county's economy, as of all England's then, was the land. The face of the countryside was not, for the most part, so very different from what it is today. Some enclosures went on during the eighteenth century, turning the old big common fields into smaller ones set about with hedges—the familiar patch-work we see everywhere now ; but the open-field system was never universal in Somerset, as it was in the Midlands.

[1] *Proceedings of the Somerset Archæological Society*, lv. 45-6 ; Collinson, *History of Somerset* (1791), ii. 186.

There are, however, two exceptions to this statement—two big areas in which very considerable changes did take place during this period. There was first the draining and enclosing of the flat plain, Brent Marsh and Sedgemoor. This great project had twice been attempted in the seventeenth century, without success. It was not taken seriously in hand until the last quarter of the eighteenth. More than 20,000 acres of Brent Marsh were enclosed in these years, and some 16,000 of Sedgemoor, besides a good deal of the smaller marshes further south, round Athelney and Langport. At the same time, too, large tracts of the high ground to the north, on the Mendip slopes, were also enclosed. By these operations the value of the land was greatly increased, in some cases three or four-fold.[1]

And secondly these years see the beginning of the reclamation of Exmoor—a magnificent story of the imagination and courage of one man. The idea of turning this huge region of waste land to profitable use was first suggested in 1795.[2] Nothing was done about it for twenty years. Then, in 1815, an Act was passed for its enclosure, and in 1818 that part of it which was Crown land—some 10,000 acres—was sold to John Knight, a Worcestershire landlord who had already made some experiments in reclaiming heath land in his own county. By 1820, after two further purchases, Knight had become the owner of 15,000 acres of Exmoor.

At that time there was one house and a homestead at Simonsbath, and not another house on the whole estate ; the Moor boasted exactly thirty-nine trees ; the so-called roads that crossed it were no more than grass-covered tracks.

[1] J. Billingsley, *General View of the Agriculture of the County of Somerset* (ed. 3, 1798), 12, 48, 76, 77, 189-97, 204. This estimate of the increase in value appears to be a very cautious one. Richard Locke claimed that the average value of land on Sedgemoor had been raised, by enclosure, from 2s. 6d. to £1 14s. an acre : *Supplement to Collinson's History of Somerset*, ed. Miss F. M. Ward (1939) 130.
[2] Billingsley, 286-9.

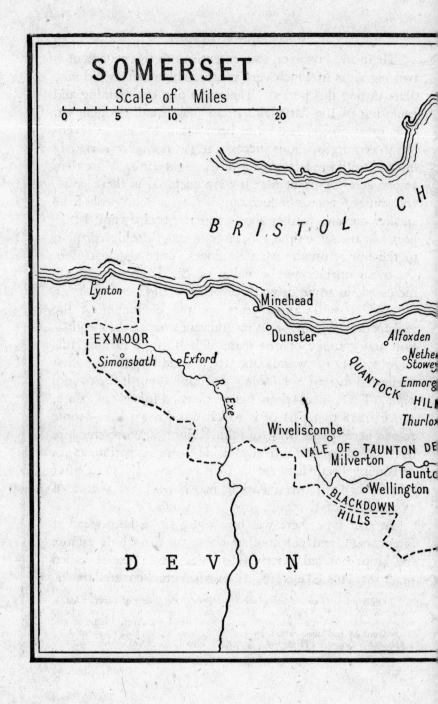

SOMERSET

Scale of Miles

0    5    10              20

BRISTOL    CH

Lynton

Minehead

EXMOOR

Dunster

Alfoxden

Simonsbath    Exford

Nethe
Stowey

QUANTOCK

Enmorg

HILL

R. Exe

Thurlox

Wiveliscombe

VALE OF TAUNTON DE

Milverton

Taunto

Wellington

BLACKDOWN
HILLS

DEVON

It was fit for one thing only : to provide grazing for the flocks of sheep, driven there in great numbers every summer from the surrounding parishes of Somerset and Devon.

John Knight set himself to change all this, and even within the period we are considering he brought about great improvements. He began by building a great wall round the whole of his property, twenty-nine miles long. It was finished by 1824. At the same time he took the roads in hand. He metalled the road from Exford to Simonsbath, and the road over Brendon Common to Lynton was also his work. He built a few homesteads in the 1820s, began to bring some of the more sheltered parts of the Moor into tillage, imported cattle from Hereford and Scotland, bred horses and improved the breed of the native ponies. All this was only a beginning. The rest of the story, with its exciting experiments and failures, belongs properly to Victorian Somerset ; and it has been admirably told by Dr. Orwin.[1]

John Knight was far from being the only improving landlord in the county. Somerset was not eminently distinguished, it is true, for its contributions to agricultural knowledge in the eighteenth century, as Leicestershire and Norfolk were. But Lord Somerville, who was born and lived much of his life at Fitzhead Court near Milverton, claims a place in the history of English agriculture, especially for his notable improvements in sheep-breeding, and Richard Locke deserves to be remembered also for his work as an advocate of enclosure and of new agricultural methods. " Agricultural improvements dictated by wisdom and pursued by industry," he wrote, " will make Somersetshire the paradise of England and England the garden of Europe."[2]  The Bath Agricultural Society,

[1] C. S. Orwin, *The Reclamation of Exmoor Forest* (1929), 10, 15, 18-33, 38, 40-8.
[2] *Supplement to Collinson's History of Somerset*, 98.

too, which was founded in 1778, did valuable work in spreading knowledge of new methods.[1] It had its smaller counterparts : the Wiveliscombe Agricultural Society, for example, which was established in 1798, and offered prizes for ploughing, for sheep-shearing, as well as one to the man who planted " the largest amount of land within ten miles of Wiveliscombe to corn or other vegetables ".[2] (Remember it was war-time, and there was the same urgent need for growing more food as we ourselves have experienced in recent years.)

The most fertile agricultural land was all in the south of the county. Flax and hemp were grown round Wincanton and Crewkerne ; the market at Chard on Mondays was said to be the largest market for potatoes in England ; the best barley came from Weston Zoyland and the other parishes on the south side of Sedgemoor, the best cider from the Vale of Taunton Dean.[3] Somerton was the centre of a rich market-gardening district ; and it was particularly noticed that it supplied " the adjacent markets even so far as Wells and Shepton Mallet with early peas, beans, potatoes, etc., and in the month of August with cucumbers by cart-loads ".[4] " Even so far as Wells and Shepton Mallet " : neither of those towns is as much as fifteen miles from Somerton, yet it was thought remarkable that those vegetables should be carried all that way. Here is a good illustration of the static life people led then —static to a degree it is hard for us to imagine now, the railway and the motor-car have made such a great revolution in our habits of thought.

In the eighteenth century you were almost entirely dependent upon your immediate neighbourhood for your

---

[1] Collinson, *History of Somerset*, i (Bath section), 79.
[2] F. Hancock, *Wifela's Combe* (1911), 189-92.
[3] Billingsley, 198, 213, 282 ; Collinson, ii. 472.
[4] Billingsley, 200.

food, your servants, your society. A man could get about on horseback, and his radius for ordinary visiting might be something like fifteen miles. Women had to be content with less : a very few miles indeed in a carriage or coach, and then only by day or on moonlit nights. Even this was much curtailed in winter. In really bad weather everybody but lunatics and people on urgent business stayed at home.

It was not until late in the century that the roads began to show any real improvement, and then only the trunk roads were affected. The great main road through Somerset followed very closely the track of the modern Western Region railway line, coming into the county a little east of Bruton and then passing through Castle Cary, Somerton, Langport, and Taunton to leave it again just beyond Wellington. Another took the same route as the Southern line today, through Milborne Port, Yeovil, and Crewkerne, and so on to Axminster and Exeter.[1] The roads between Bristol and Bath were excellent—one of them is said to have been the first to be " macadamised " in England— and they were continued by two fine roads to London.

The other roads, however, were deplorable. The middle section of the road from Glastonbury to Taunton, before Sedgemoor was drained, was described by a guide-book in 1786 as " only a summer road, then not good for a carriage " ; and similarly, forty years later, the road from Bridgwater to South Molton was " impassable in winter, but pleasant in summer ".[2] Minehead, tucked away in a corner of the county, shut in by hills, was almost inaccessible to wheeled traffic. " No mail, stage-coach, or waggon sets out from hence ", says a directory of the end of the century. Instead, the place was dependent upon " three common stage-carts " a week, one each to Bristol, Taunton,

---

[1] Paterson's *Roads* (ed. 7, 1786), 32, 45.
[2] Paterson's *Roads* (ed. 7, 1786), 183 ; ibid. (ed. 18, 1829), 82.

CROWCOMBE COURT (1734)

From a drawing by J. Buckler (1835) in the collection of the
Somersetshire Archæological Society at Taunton Castle

THE PYNSENT COLUMN AND BURTON PYNSENT
From an engraving by T. Bonnor in Collinson's
*History of Somerset* (1791)

and Tiverton. There was also a thrice-weekly post as far as Taunton.[1]

Travelling was not only difficult and uncomfortable. It was expensive. You could get about fairly cheaply on horseback : young Woodforde, returning from Ansford (near Castle Cary) to Oxford after the long vacation of 1760, did the journey in two days for 17s. 9d. for himself and his horse. But look at what it cost him later on, when he had risen in the world to become a Fellow of New College and could afford to travel in comfort. In 1774 he hired a post-chaise and did the whole run in a day : it cost him £4 8s. Two years later he again took a post-chaise and indulged himself by spending the night at Tetbury : his expenses were £5 9s. 5d.[2]

The Georgian age draws to an end with the triumph of the stage and the mail-coach. It was brilliant, but it lasted only a short time before the railways came in and swept every competing kind of transport out of their way. Still, the coaches have left their memory behind them : physically, in the great hotels that were built to cater for their passengers, with their noble façades and fine public rooms—the County Hotel at Taunton, or the Clarence at Bridgwater—and the humbler road-side inns, like that delightful one at Temple Cloud on the road from Bristol to Wells. The coaches ought to be remembered, too, for their names, which call them back to us, I think, as nothing else can. What about these, a sample, taken almost at random, of those that passed through Bridgwater —*Royal Devonshire, Estafette, John o'Groat, Nonpareil, Swiftsure* ?[3]

But the stage-coaches benefited only passengers and the Post Office. They did nothing to improve or speed up the

[1] F. Hancock, *Minehead* (1903), 10-11.
[2] *The Diary of a Country Parson*, i (1924), 15, 131, 174.
[3] A. H. Powell, *Bridgwater in the Later Days* (1908), 160-1.

conveyance of heavy goods, which continued to be carried by pack-horse and cart, as they had been carried in the Middle Ages. The eighteenth century did, however, make a material contribution to the quicker and easier transport of goods by the great development it gave to the system of English waterways. In Somerset it started in Queen Anne's reign, when an Act was secured for making the Avon navigable up to Bath.[1] In the closing decade of the century the canal mania seized upon Somerset, and several important plans were launched—not to mention a host of frivolous schemes that never had a chance of realisation from the beginning. Of those that were successfully carried out, wholly or in part, the most important was the Kennet and Avon Canal, running from Bath to Newbury. Since the Kennet had already been made navigable from Newbury to Reading, where it falls into the Thames, this canal afforded through communication by water between the Bristol Channel and London and the North Sea. It was a really great work, authorised in 1794 and completed in 1810.[2] It contributed substantially to the development of the Somerset coal-field, for a feeder was built to it (known as the Somerset Coal Canal), running from Paulton to join the Kennet and Avon Canal near Limpley Stoke. This was opened in 1798.[3]

Railways, also, appeared in Somerset in the eighteenth century, and with the same purpose: the carriage of heavy goods, not of passengers. They were indeed intimately connected with the development of water transport. The earliest of them was that built by Ralph Allen to convey the stone from his quarries on Combe Down to the river Avon, newly made navigable. Notice

---

[1] Collinson, i (Bath section), 28.
[2] Phelps, *History of Somersetshire* (1839), i. 59 n.
[3] *Somerset and Dorset Notes and Queries*, xxiv. 177; *Proc. Som. Arch. Soc.*, xxxviii. 353 sq.

that Allen was treasurer of the Avon Navigation, that barges began to use the river in 1727, and that his little railway was already in operation by 1730.[1] Again, the Coal Canal owned lines of railway, which it was authorised to build by Acts of Parliament between 1794 and 1802 : the chief of them ran from Radstock down to the canal near Limpley Stoke.[2]

These were no more than modest beginnings, forerunners of the railway in the full modern sense of the term : a public line, that is, open to all for the conveyance of both passengers and goods by mechanical traction. For that Somerset had to wait until 31 August 1840, when the section of the Great Western Railway from Bristol to Bath was opened.

But even so, these improvements in transport by land and water were very considerable, taken all together—much more important than any that had been seen in the county since the Romans built their roads there. They did much to foster its trade. We have already seen how eager the proprietors of the coal-field were to take advantage of canals and railways : so much so that the conservatively-minded took fright. At the end of the eighteenth century a contemporary noted that " many people are under alarming apprehensions lest the coal-mines may be exhausted by the extra demand produced by the extension of sale established by the canals ". But he hastens to reassure the nervous " that more than treble the present quantity could be raised from the pits already in use, did the demand require it ; and the increased quantity might be supplied for several hundred years ".[3]

In the course of the period we are dealing with, the centres of the Somerset coal-field shifted. Previously there

[1] C. E. Lee, *The Evolution of Railways* (ed. 2, 1943), 43-9.
[2] Phelps, i. 59 ; C. and J. Greenwood, *Somersetshire Delineated* (1822), 198.
[3] Billingsley, 30.

had been two main areas of production : one immediately outside Bristol, in the parishes of Brislington and Queen Charlton, the other much further to the south, round Farrington Gurney. Early in the eighteenth century there were rumours of coal at Radstock, but they were discountenanced by the wiseacres. An old collier was in the habit of saying that " if ever coal was found in Radstock he would get on the top of Norton tower and *flee* down ".[1] It is to be hoped that he was dead by 1763, for in that year coal *was* found at Radstock, in such quantity that the little town soon became the headquarters of the whole field, and by the beginning of the nineteenth century the Brislington pits and most of those round Pensford and Farrington Gurney had shut down. At that time the total coal-production of Somerset was reckoned at about 140,000 tons a year : a substantial quantity—half as much again as that of the Forest of Dean—but still not very large when set beside the ten million tons then produced by the whole of Great Britain.[2] And in spite of the marked improvement in transport, the Somerset coal-field could not compete with the great fields of the Midlands and the North in supplying the needs of London and the new mechanised industry. Somerset coal did not find its way far afield : it was almost entirely absorbed by the city of Bath, the villages of Somerset itself, and the neighbouring counties of Wiltshire and Dorset.

The characteristic industry of Somerset had long been the manufacture of woollens, the centre of which in Defoe's time was Frome, a town whose prosperity made a deep impression on him. " If their trade continues to increase for a few years more, as it has done for those past," he noted, " it is very likely to be one of the greatest and

---

[1] Quoted in *Victoria County History of Somerset*, ii. 384.
[2] Billingsley, 27, 29. Cf. J. U. Nef, *Rise of the British Coal Industry* (1932), i. 20, and Appendix B.

HAMMET STREET, TAUNTON (1778), LOOKING UP TO ST. MARY'S CHURCH

From an engraving in Toulmin's
*History of Taunton* (1791)

THE MARKET HOUSE, TAUNTON (1772)

From a drawing by J. Buckler (1835) in the collection of the
Somersetshire Archæological Society at Taunton Castle

wealthiest inland towns in England."[1]   It did go on
increasing for a time, though never so as to fulfil the whole
of Defoe's prophecy.   But about the end of the century its
advance halted ;  and then, slowly, the trade of Frome
began to decline.   When Cobbett saw the town, he took
an instant dislike to it.   He called it—and few terms in
his vocabulary were more insulting—" a sort of little
Manchester.  A very small Manchester indeed ;  for it does
not contain above ten to twelve thousand people, but it
has all the *flash* of a Manchester, and the innkeepers and
their people look and behave like their Manchester fellows.
I was, I must confess, glad to find proofs of the irretriev-
able decay of the place ".[2]

Frome's decline was shared by the whole neighbourhood.   It was no more than a symptom of the general
decline of the West-Country woollen industry.   In the face
of it some towns took to new manufactures :  Taunton
tried silk in 1778, Yeovil had already begun to make
gloves when Defoe was there.[3]   The change-over was not
rapid—the woollen industry has not wholly left the county
even now.   But in the eighteenth century the West Country
yielded up to the North its old pre-eminence :  while
Bradford and Leeds shot forward, the Somerset towns
stood still.

Substantial domestic industries remained, however, in
the villages, for which the towns usually provided headquarters and markets.   The making of sail-cloth in the
country round Yeovil, for instance.   The industry was well
established in the eighteenth century.   It reached its greatest
boom during the Napoleonic war, when the navy was
willing to consume almost all that Somerset could supply ;
but even with the return of peace the manufacture con-

[1] *Tour through England and Wales* (Everyman ed.), i. 280.
[2] *Rural Rides* (" Everyman " ed.), ii. 72.
[3] J. Toulmin, *History of Taunton* (1874 ed.), 333 ;  Defoe, *Tour*, i. 218.

tinued, at least till the 1870s, and in the town of Crewkerne it lasted much longer.[1]

The maritime trade of the county had become of very little importance by the end of the eighteenth century. Minehead, which subsisted chiefly on imports from Ireland and the West Indies, did fairly well in the 1750s and 1760s, but its trade then fell off, swallowed up, like that of the whole Bristol Channel, by the ever-growing city of Bristol itself.[2] Here, as everywhere else, one sees the dominant position held by Bristol, and to a lesser degree by Bath, in the economy of Somerset. The two cities were engrossing much of the county's trade, as of its agricultural produce : the butchers of Bath and Bristol went down to Shepton Mallet to buy calves, bringing them back over the Mendips in carts ; and in 1816 we are told that the fish-market at Bath, held three times a week, " far excels that of any inland town in the kingdom ".[3]

There, then, is a sketch of some of the chief features of the economy of Somerset under the Georges. What about the life of its people, their material condition, their feelings and ideas ? There is the heart of my subject.

As to the poor—the great majority of the people of Somerset—we can give only a very inadequate answer to those questions. We know so little that is of any real value, when all is said, about the inner working of their minds ; for they remained inarticulate and they found few sympathetic interpreters. But we have a good deal of evidence about their material condition, and occasionally something more intimately revealing has been preserved for us.

[1] *Proc. Som. Arch. Soc.*, lxxvi. 15 ; *V. C. H.* ii. 424-5 ; *Supplement to Collinson's History of Somerset*, 104.
[2] Ibid., 112-13 ; Hancock, *Minehead*, 316-17.
[3] Billingsley, 248 n. ; T. H. B. Oldfield, *Representative History of Great Britain* (1816), iv. 419.

For almost the whole of the eighteenth century the average labourer's wage in Somerset stood unchanged at a shilling a day, usually with an allowance of beer or cider in addition. In the summer, and especially at harvest-time, the wage might rise to 1s. 4d.[1] It was only in the closing decade of the century that any general increase appeared, and then it was far from sufficient to keep pace with the great rise in prices that had been going on for more than twenty years past. Consider the price of wheat alone. In 1776 it stood in Somerset at about 35s. a quarter ; in 1793, at the beginning of the long war with France, it was 48s. ; in 1795 and 1796, which were years of terrible scarcity and hardship, it rocketed up to 112s.—more than three times what it had been twenty years earlier ; and though it halved itself the next year, the price remained almost prohibitive for the really poor for many years to come.[2] The price of other necessary provisions also rose steadily, though less spectacularly.

The closing years of the eighteenth century, and the first half of the nineteenth, were a period of very general distress for the poor, in Somerset as over most of the country. The remedies tried in Somerset, the various forms of assistance paid out of the rates, once again did not differ materially from those used elsewhere in southern England. The account given by historians of the administration of poor relief in these years has usually represented Authority (central and local) as puzzled and frightened and harsh. Puzzled and frightened it certainly was, and the result was a muddle, shocking inefficiency and waste : but though there was plenty of harshness, there was plenty of well-meant kindness too, and that has received rather less attention, I think, than it deserves.

[1] Hancock, *Dunster Church and Priory* (1905), 158 (wage in 1718); *V. C. H.* ii. 321 (wage in 1771) ; Billingsley, 152, 259, 294.
[2] *V. C. H.* ii. 321 ; Billingsley, 152-3.

It comes out clearly, again and again, in the accounts of the parochial Overseers of the Poor. Sometimes they were obviously ogres. But, on the other hand, consider some of the things the Overseers did for the poor under their care in the parish of Kilmersdon. They paid apprentices' premiums ; they repaired the cottages of the poor, and even paid their rents ; they supplied medical attention when it was needed and conveyed serious cases to hospital at Bristol or Bath ; they hired watchers for the bed-sides of the sick. Altogether, Lord Hylton concludes in his history of the parish that " the Overseers erred rather in being too generous than the reverse ".[1]

Or again, take an example from the parochial accounts of Swainswick, in the reign of George I. In them we can trace the career of a bastard boy, for whose upbringing the parish was responsible. He was born in 1716 and was presumably a foundling. A good deal of money was spent in trying to find the child's mother : the town criers at Marshfield and Bath were employed, but to no purpose. The parish then had the child baptised and resigned itself to the cost of his maintenance. Thenceforward for the next eight years " George the base child " takes a leading place in the parish accounts—whether it is for caps and hose and breeches and shoes, for his keep, for mending his clothes, for his schooling, or finally for binding him out apprentice to a gardener (£6 for this last, in 1725 : a substantial sum).[2]

Instances of the same sort could easily be multiplied. I confine myself to these two. I am not concerned to defend the old administration of poor relief : the Act of 1834 that swept it away was a great measure of reform,

---

[1] Lord Hylton, *History of Kilmersdon* (1910), 169.
[2] R. E. M. Peach, *Annals of the Parish of Swainswick* (1890), 155-8.

drastic but necessary. I only wish to point out that it
had its good side, that many of those who were responsible
for the welfare of the poor showed themselves genuinely
ready to help them. You see it again in other ways. At
Wells, for instance, in 1826 Bishop Law turned fifty
acres of his land into allotments, which were let to
the poor at a low rent. The results, it was noted, were
most gratifying for every one. Many of the holders of the
allotments were now able to keep themselves without
applying for relief; the Bishop was popular, his pheasants
were not poached, and in the time of riots that preceded
the Reform Bill—when in Bristol the bishop's palace
was burnt down—the labourers at Wells spontaneously
offered to defend the palace from any violence that might
threaten it.[1]

The mention of those riots reminds us of the turbulence
of the English people in the eighteenth century, to be
seen in Somerset as elsewhere up and down the country.
It would be a mistake to suppose that the people accepted
hard times without any protest—and what protest could
they offer but rioting? In 1801 Thomas Poole reported
to Coleridge from Nether Stowey that trouble was wide-
spread throughout his district. " The men of Stogursey
and the neighbouring parishes ", he said, " joined the
people here and patrolled the country. They committed
no violence, indeed they met with no opposition." And
for the moment their protest was effective : they forced
the price of provisions down.[2] That was a moderate,
peaceful demonstration. It was not always so. The introduction of machinery, for instance, often acted as an incite-
ment to violence from those who thought it threatened
their employment : as at Shepton Mallet in 1776, when the

[1] V. C. H. ii. 330.
[2] Mrs. Sandford, *Thomas Poole and his Friends* (1888), ii. 42-3.

cloth-workers destroyed new machines that had just been installed.[1]

The people of Shepton Mallet seem, indeed, to have been distinguished for their rowdiness. John Wesley had a narrow escape when he preached there in February 1748. A mob had been " hired, prepared and made sufficiently drunk, in order to do all manner of mischief ". Wesley was pursued with stones in the streets, and the mob broke into the house where he was staying. It was their intention to set it on fire, until they discovered that he had escaped by a back door. All the same, one must add that when he next came to Shepton, in 1753, he " found much life among the poor, plain people ", and " a little loving society " formed itself there, drawn almost entirely from the poor.[2]

The general picture, then, of the condition of the poor in this period is one of sufficiency, changing late in the eighteenth century into hardship and then, very often, to real distress, tempered by the more or less sympathetic administration of an inefficient system of poor relief. And of course by private charity too. For it was a very charitable age—look at the boards so frequently displayed in churches, preserving the names of the parish benefactors and the nature of their good deeds. The tradition had descended from the sixteenth and seventeenth centuries, and it was worthily maintained in the eighteenth. Especially perhaps in one direction: the improvement of the education of the poor.

As you go down from the market-place at Frome to the river, just by the bridge you come upon a tall, rather elegant classical building. It is crowned by a bell-turret: in the centre of the façade is the figure of a dame, leaning

---

[1] V. C. H. ii. 417.
[2] Wesley, Journal (Everyman ed.), ii. 45-7, 282, 427.

on her stick, and below her a neat school-child. This is the Blue-coat School, and the history of its establishment is instructive. A subscription for forming it was set on foot about the year 1720, and it quickly reached the great sum of £1,087. The school was then built and endowed for the purpose of teaching twenty boys the three Rs and the principles of the Church of England, maintaining and clothing them at the same time, and finally apprenticing them to some trade. When Collinson wrote seventy years later, the school was carried on in exactly the same way, the master receiving a salary of £24 a year.[1] There were many more such schools in the county : one founded at Chewstoke in 1718, for example, another at Minehead about 1767. Later in the century we come to Hannah More's famous schools in Wrington and its neighbourhood, and more modest efforts too, such as that of Tom Poole's cousin John at Enmore, and the school at Nether Stowey started in a room built for the purpose by Tom Poole himself in 1813.[2]

The effects of such measures as these were slow to appear, and they are difficult for us to estimate with accuracy now. There was a good deal of ostentation, and some cant, in eighteenth-century charity. We are apt to view it unsympathetically today, in a wholly different social order, as something condescendingly done for the poor by the wealthy, the work of a succession of Lady Bountifuls, moved by the itch to interfere in other people's concerns and sometimes by the twinges of a guilty conscience. But I think that is a wrong view. The eighteenth century contributed a good deal more than we usually allow towards humanising the life of the poor : that was not wholly due

[1] Collinson, ii. 197.
[2] Collinson, ii. 94 ; Hancock, *Minehead*, 40 ; Sandford, *Thomas Poole*, ii. 124, 266-7.

to the Victorians, with their more efficient, systematic
legislation. The work, in particular, of Wesley and his
followers left the strongest marks behind it, in civilising
—in the broadest sense of the word—the people to whom
it was addressed. How could it have been otherwise,
when Wesley formed his steady, eager following among
the " honest colliers " of Coleford, whom he called " the
most numerous as well as the most lively society in
Somersetshire " ? It was always a pleasure to him to go
there, and obviously for them to hear him. " I went on ",
he wrote in September 1782 (the wonderful man was
already seventy-nine), " to the simple-hearted colliers at
Coleford, abundance of whom met at six in the evening
in a green meadow, which was delightfully gilded by the
rays of the setting sun."[1]

That leads us on to a consideration of the religious
life of Georgian Somerset : in particular, the life and work
of the Anglican church. Here again we are up against a
good deal of misunderstanding, of misinterpretation to
my mind, in the past. To the Victorians almost everything
the eighteenth century did was wrong. They found it
cool where they themselves were enthusiastic, they disapproved of its morals, they hated its taste. They did their
best to obliterate all trace of its work, and they set themselves—in perfect good faith—to decry and blacken its
achievement. Nowhere is this seen more clearly than in
the matter of religion. All the instincts of the Victorians
were unsympathetic to the quiet, sober, practical religion
of their grandfathers : they found the Georgian Church
corrupt, apathetic, tasteless, smug. We are only just
beginning to question that verdict, and the more closely
one considers it the more strongly one comes to doubt its
justice.

[1] Wesley, *Journal*, ii. 397, iv. 242.

It is often said, truly enough, that many of the Georgian clergy were pluralists. In that they resembled their predecessors in the seventeenth century, in the sixteenth, in the Middle Ages. The conception of a wholly resident clergy—one man one living—is Victorian, and it demanded a great adjustment of clerical incomes before it could be achieved. That readjustment went on, energetically, in the eighteenth century, in the augmentation of livings, designed to bring up the poorer stipends to a sum on which a clergyman could decently maintain himself. It is not always realised what a remarkable effort was made towards this end, from Queen Anne's Bounty and by private benefaction, before ever Queen Victoria came to the throne. In the diocese of Bath and Wells by 1833 the enormous sum of £3,300,000 had already been applied to this purpose, and the average value of livings was stated to be £250 a year—a sum substantially higher, in relation to the purchasing power of money, than the average value of livings in the Church of England today.[1] It would be absurd to deny that pluralism was wide spread among Georgian parsons, but the evil was recognised and the first, essential step had already been taken towards lessening, and even ultimately doing away with it altogether. The more conscientious of the clergy were fully alive to the scandal. Dr. Majendie, for example (who afterwards became Bishop of Chester), was vicar of Nether Stowey from 1790 to 1793. When he was appointed to the vicarage of Hungerford in Berkshire he insisted on resigning Nether Stowey, since he disapproved of holding two livings at once.[2]

It is right, I think, to recognise that the average Georgian parson did his duty adequately and conscientiously by the standards of his time—and it would surely be unfair to

[1] Phelps, i. 106, 121.
[2] D. N. B.; Sandford, *Thomas Poole*, i. 59-61.

judge him by any other standards. He performed services twice on Sundays, administered the Holy Communion four times a year as a rule, and did his parish rounds. Many clergymen did a great deal more than that, then as now, and tributes of affection to their memory survive, from that age as from this : whether it is at Martock to the Rev. Thomas Bowyer, the indefatigable parson of the parish for 55 years ; or at Stanton Drew, where it was noted on a monument to the Rev. Samuel Prigg, vicar for half a century, that " he was constantly resident, and so zealous a performer of his duty that even the extreme severity of the winter in 1739 could not deter him from persevering in it though then eighty years old, by which he contracted an illness that put a period to his well-spent life, 1740 ".[1]

By a happy chance, we are able to learn something of this good side of eighteenth-century clerical life from a number of diaries that have survived ; and two in particular —those of James Woodforde and John Skinner. *The Diary of a Country Parson* has become a famous book in the last twenty-five years : it has made the name of " Parson Woodforde " very widely known. The greater part of it is concerned with Norfolk, where Woodforde held a living from 1776 to his death in 1803. But he came originally from Somerset—his father was rector of Ansford and vicar of Castle Cary, two adjacent parishes ; and his diary has a good deal to tell us of the life of that part of the county. Woodforde's own clerical career began, too, in Somerset curacies : Thurloxton, near Taunton, Babcary, Castle Cary. He was generally paid £20 or £30 a year, took the Easter offerings and the surplice fees himself, and received the use of the parsonage, its gardens and stables.[2] He would

---

[1] *Notes and Queries for Somerset and Dorset*, xxiv. 144-5 ; Collinson, ii. 435.
[2] *Diary of a Country Parson*, i. 33.

take a morning and an afternoon service on Sundays, besides services on holy days and such special occasions as 30 January and 5 November. But though he performed his duties sufficiently, he could not be a true substitute for a resident parson: he remained a visitor to the parish.

His personality emerges very clearly for us from his diary: easy-going, tolerant, kindly, fond of animals, a man of very moderate abilities, no great reader and nothing of a scholar. Coursing a hare and fishing were his chief pleasures—and eating; for every reader of the diary will remember his meticulous care in describing the meals of the day, his solemn respect for good food.

In almost every one of these characteristics Parson Skinner of Camerton was his exact opposite. He too was a kind man by nature, but long ill luck and misunderstanding sharpened his temper and overlaid his kindliness. He was so much that Woodforde was not: a scholar, an introvert, an idealist, a father—yes, a great deal of his trouble came from that, for he constantly quarrelled with his children. He was also a notably conscientious man, worried by infidelity, by Methodism, by the moral delinquencies of his parishioners. But if one may say it without being heartless, his misfortunes have turned to our gain: for they led him to confide more and more fully in his diary as the years went by, until at last it becomes one of the most touching records of a tormented spirit that we have.

Everything was out of joint for poor Skinner. He should have had a canonry, or some quiet country living, with the freedom to pursue his antiquarian researches, which might possibly have led to some valuable result. Instead, he found himself among the coal-miners of Camerton, ageing, disillusioned, quarrelsome, sensitive to every kind of slight, real and imagined (he had to put up with both). In the end it was all too much for him, and he shot himself in February 1839.

There, then, are two Somerset clergymen of this age, known to us from the mere accident that they kept diaries that have survived. Neither of them corresponds to the traditional picture of a Georgian parson—a fat pluralist, useless and lazy, or an illiterate Parson Trulliber, with his heart in his pig-sty.

It would be equally wrong to accept without reserve the Victorians' estimate of the way in which their Georgian predecessors looked after and maintained their churches. It is perfectly true that the fabrics often needed much more repair than they received : alas ! for it was this that made the way for the " restorer ", who swept off as rubbish so much that we should have liked preserved. But a great deal was done in the eighteenth century to keep the fabrics in order. Let us take the church of Chew Magna as an example. In 1733 £27 was spent on leading the roof and glazing the windows ; £114 more two years later—this included a great deal of whitewashing and painting, as well as £80 to John Bilbie, the great bell-founder of Chew Stoke, for recasting the parish's six bells ; then in 1755 the church was repaved and largely reseated, at a cost of £138, followed the next year by painting the pews, gallery, and pulpit—£20.[1] And so it goes on, all through the century. The fabric was certainly not neglected.

More than this. The men of the eighteenth century did a great deal towards the beautification of their churches. Think of those candelabra they loved, for instance : the fine set at Ilminster, given by William Raw in 1762 ; or the glorious one at Axbridge, made in Bristol in 1729 (it

[1] F. A. Wood, *Collections for a Parochial History of Chew Magna* (1903), 234-6.

cost nearly £23 all told, by the time it was set up in the church : no wonder the vestry meeting had felt nervous about undertaking the expense).[1]  Or listen to the contemporary historian Collinson on the church of Martock. It has a splendid nave, one of the best works of the fifteenth century in the whole county.  But " what renders this church a subject of general admiration is an elegant superb altar-piece in stucco plaster, erected at the sole expense of John Butler esq. as a testimony of his regard and affection for the church and place of his nativity." It is interesting, by the way, to notice who this John Butler was—a colonial, a leading inhabitant of Nova Scotia. Already the colonists were beginning to display that affection for England which became so familiar in the course of the nineteenth century.

Not many new churches were built in Somerset in these years—and of those that were built very few have survived unaltered. The county can show nothing like the array of Georgian churches in Shropshire, or the delightful little group in East Leicestershire and Rutland. The most important of those that survive are perhaps two in the Frome district—Babington and Berkley, with its delicate plaster ceiling ;  and Wiveliscombe, a Regency Gothic church of 1827-1829.[2] But besides these there is one piece of Georgian ecclesiastical architecture in the county that is of high interest : the chancel of the church at Bruton. This was built by the Hon. Charles Berkeley in 1743, to replace a very small chancel of the fourteenth century. It is clear that Mr. Berkeley and his architect[3] considered the old

---

[1] Axbridge churchwardens' accounts.

[2] M. Whiffen, *Stuart and Georgian Churches outside London* (1948), 45, 71 ;  *Proc. Som. Arch. Soc.*, lxxxiii. 54-7.

[3] The chancel has been attributed to Nathaniel Ireson of Wincanton, on the authority of G. Sweetman's *History of Wincanton* (1903), 211 ; but Sweetman gives no reference for the statement. On Ireson see Mr. H. St. George Gray's paper in *Proc. Som. Arch. Soc.*, lxxxvii. 81-4.

chancel wholly unworthy of the superb Perpendicular nave to which it was attached, and that they wished to make an eastern termination to the church as fine—in its different, classical style—as the rest of this late Gothic building. Beyond doubt they succeeded. The chancel at Bruton is one of the most charming things we have in that rare and delicate style—the chaste English baroque.

All sorts of things call for remark in it. I limit myself to two. First, the astonishing way in which it blends with the Gothic nave. Again and again, in different ways, one notices the affinity between Perpendicular and classical architecture, both in design and in spirit. Nowhere is that seen better than at Bruton. As you look up the nave to the east end for the first time you get a momentary surprise— for this is something very uncommon indeed ; but directly you become accustomed to it, it will strike you how little there is that is incongruous between these two pieces of building, the nave of the fifteenth and sixteenth centuries, the chancel of the eighteenth.

And then as you go up into the chancel itself you see the full beauty of its decoration. The elliptical stone-vaulted roof, with its elaborate floral bosses (a medieval idea, of course), the whole thing painted now in faded, delicate blue and lemon and pink and cream. Then, in contrast to this riotous roof, the plain severe Georgian floor and fittings : the black and white pavement, the unpainted box pews. And finally the east end : the mahogany altar-rails, the splendid plaster reredos, IHS in a glory in the middle, a cornucopia at each side—the details of the carved flowers differing, for this is a subtle work, with no merely mechanical repetitions.

I have chosen to speak of the chancel at Bruton because it is something of exceptional merit : it would not be too much to say that it shows a Georgian architect working under inspiration. We cannot be sufficiently thankful that it has been preserved to us, that it was not destroyed by the Victorian restorer of the church. It was not for lack of the will : he actually prepared plans for replacing it with a Gothic chancel of his own—but whether the funds ran out or some influential parishioner forbade it, the rebuilding never came off.[1] It was a great mercy.

If we except the city of Bath and its immediate neighbourhood, Somerset is not very rich in notable Georgian building. It cannot claim a single first-class Georgian country house, except Prior Park. Perhaps one should add Enmore Castle, south-west of Bridgwater, a remarkable essay in medievalism, put up by the second Earl of Egmont, who died in 1770. The only entrance to it was through a gateway defended by a drawbridge, and Horace Walpole maliciously noted that the Earl (who was a well-known eccentric) had " prepared it to defend itself with crossbows and arrows, against the time in which the fabric and use of gunpowder shall be forgotten ".[2] But that was a freak. The nobility and gentry of Georgian Somerset preferred as a rule to add discreetly to their existing house—as the Luttrells did, for instance, at Dunster and the Phelipses at Montacute. Hence it is that we find very little work here done by any of the great eighteenth-century architects, though there are many pleasant houses by country builders, such as Ireson's delightful Crowcombe Court. I am not aware of any building in the county that can certainly be ascribed to Gibbs or the Adam brothers—though Sir William Chambers is said to have reconstructed the east wing of Coker Court, and James Wyatt built Ammerdown House near Radstock.[3]

[1] *Proc. Som. Arch. Soc.*, lxxix. 6 ; G. W. O. Addleshaw and F. Etchells, *The Architectural Setting of Anglican Worship* (1948), 158 n.
[2] *Memoirs of the Reign of George III* (1845), i. 388.
[3] J. Batten, *Historical and Topographical Collections relating to . . . South Somerset* (1894), 159 ; Lord Hylton, *History of Kilmersdon*, 60.

No. The greater gentry left their mark on eighteenth-
century Somerset in other ways : most notably by re-
fashioning so much of the county's landscape, their careful
and discriminating plantations. They had, too, a special
fondness for monuments, the towers and columns that
still crown and adorn the Somerset hills. Look at those
three splendid monuments in the south of the county :
Alfred's Tower above Bruton, just inside the border from
Wiltshire, the Pynsent Column erected by Chatham, the
Wellington monument on the Blackdown Hills. I always
look up for them as I pass by in the train and think of
Chatham, as it were, calling to Wellington across the great
Taunton levels.

Much good Georgian building survives in the county,
in houses of the lesser gentry and yeomen, and in small
town houses too. There is Hammet Street in Taunton, for
instance—an excellent plain street of red-brick houses,
built in 1778, to lead up to the great church. In its austere
way, this is one of the very best eighteenth-century streets
I know : matched by one rather like it at Newark in
Nottinghamshire, but hardly to be surpassed outside Bath
and Bristol and London. Or again, consider the civic
architecture of the age. The Market House at Taunton is
an obvious example, completed in 1772 and a little injured,
I am sorry to say, in the twentieth century. More beautiful
—indeed a delightful little building—is the town hall
at Wells, which also dates from the 1770s. It was no easy
architectural feat to rebuild a whole side of that delicious
square, with its two medieval gateways and the row of
charming shops on the north side : if it had to be done
in our own time, we should be justifiably nervous of the
result. But the eighteenth century solved the problem
with all its accustomed, natural assurance, and there is
the town hall now, in snuff-coloured stone, with its pro-

The Cloisters at Wells: the south-east doorway

jecting porch and *piano nobile*, the cartouche of arms on the pediment, the bold swags at the sides : a façade that could hardly be improved.

In many ways I think one penetrates most closely to the life of Georgian Somerset in its towns. Some things, it is true, have disappeared for good. The little theatres and the travelling companies of actors for one, giving their performances in very small towns indeed. At Castle Cary (whose population barely exceeded 1,000) young Woodforde was able to see *The Beggar's Opera* and *Hamlet* and *Richard III* in 1770, and *Hamlet* again in 1773.[1] Or look at the vigorous music-making that went on in Wells earlier in the century, under the leadership of the town's chief physician, Dr. Claver Morris : the music club, meeting in the Deanery or in one of the houses in the Vicars' Close to perform the works of Handel and Purcell and Byrd. Usually they made their own music, not always very satisfactorily : " Mr. Hill's harpsichord being near a note below concert pitch, and no sure hand performing the trebles (being only young lads of Wells and Shepton), our music was very mean." How well one understands the doctor's disappointment and vexation ! But sometimes he would manage to entice an eminent professional over from Bristol or Bath, and then all criticism was silenced. " Mr. Douglas the blackmoor trumpeter (who is one of the best in England on that instrument) " came in the autumn of 1718, " and he sounded two sonatas very finely ".[2]

Such things, I am afraid, are gone for ever. I doubt if Castle Cary will see *Richard III* again, or a blackamoor trumpeter sound sonatas in Wells : the cinema and the wireless have seen to that. But, for all the superficial

[1] *Diary of a Country Parson*, i. 100, 116.
[2] *The Diary of a West-Country Physician*, ed. E. Hobhouse (ed. 3, 1935), 71, 65.

changes—the garages, the street-widening, the atrocious modern shop-fronts and the wires—it is not really difficult to recapture something of the eighteenth-century life of these towns even today. Walk along Castle Street at Bridgwater, for instance : up from the river and its old quays, at which the colliers lay, into King Square (dreadfully mangled now, but still noble) and then down to the Regency market-hall and the church behind. Are we so very far here from Defoe, who noted with approval the Nonconformist spirit of the town ; and Wesley, who disliked it—" a dead uncomfortable place at best ", he called it ;[1] and Coleridge, who preached more than once in a chapel only two or three streets away ; and Bubb Dodington, the political intriguer and borough-monger of George II's time, who represented Bridgwater in Parliament for thirty-two years and then lost the seat, after a memorable contest, in 1754 ? Turn back to that election for a moment and consider the story of it in Dodington's own words, set down with the terseness of defeat and disgust. He arrived at Bridgwater on 11 April 1754, " where, as I expected, I found things very disagreeably framed ". The next day his opponent, Lord Egmont, " came with trumpets, noise, etc." The four following days passed in electioneering—" spent in the infamous and disagreeable compliance with the low habits of venal wretches ". (Dodington had never given the electors of Bridgwater this character in all the years in which they had faithfully returned him.) Then on the 17th came the poll, " which I lost "—need it be said ?—" by the injustice of the returning officer ". A further grouse or two and then, next day, " left Bridgwater—for ever ".[2]

I am sorry to have to say that the political reputation

---

[1] Defoe, *Tour*, i. 270 ; Wesley, *Journal*, iii. 21.
[2] Dodington, *Diary* (1784), 285-6.

of Bridgwater did not improve.  Fifty years later we are told that " the contests in this borough have been productive of the grossest bribery.  We have heard of one elector boast of selling his pig for a hundred guineas and being allowed to eat it himself ;  another that he has sold his parrot for the same sum, but the candidate never claimed his purchase ".[1]  And the end of the story was the disfranchisement of the borough for corruption in 1869.  Let me hasten to add, for fear any one should misunderstand me, that I am far from wishing to cast any slur on the modern political life of Bridgwater.  I am only suggesting that so much remains of the old town still that it is really easy to think oneself back, as one walks its streets, into the vanished world of the eighteenth century.

I have now tried to recall some of the chief characteristics of the life of Georgian Somerset, a little of its atmosphere.  I have touched on a few things only, and very lightly at that.  I have said little of politics, nothing of war or of sport or of great and important industries like the Mendip mining.[2]  An adequate treatment of the subject would need a whole book, and a thick one.  But I hope I have managed to indicate something of the interest of the subject and of the wealth of material that is available for its study—not only, or even primarily, in books, but in the face of the county itself and the visible memorials of its past.

I cannot conclude, however, without referring to one other chapter in the history of Georgian Somerset, because in a sense it is the most important chapter of all, something that touches closely the minds of thousands of us today. I mean the residence of the Wordsworths and Coleridge

---

[1] Oldfield, *Representative History*, iv. 446.
[2] On this last subject see J. W. Gough, *The Mines of Mendip* (1930).

under the Quantocks in 1797 and 1798, with all its con-
sequences in the history of English literature and thought.
For it was there that the *Lyrical Ballads* were conceived,
" The Ancient Mariner " and " Kubla Khan " and
" Christabel " composed, the first preparation made towards
writing *The Prelude*, and—only a little less important—
Dorothy Wordsworth's journal begun.

It was Thomas Poole of Nether Stowey who was
responsible for bringing them down into Somerset—
Coleridge first, his special friend, to his own village, and
then the Wordsworths to Alfoxden. In his letters and in
Mrs. Sandford's charming narrative of his life we can
follow the story through his eyes—and his comments are
worth attending to, for he was a shrewd and highly
intelligent man, with a sympathetic, subtle understanding
of these men of genius who were his friends. Then,
inevitably, one turns to Dorothy Wordsworth's journal,
in which she has described for ever the life of these months
(a bare year altogether) the brief moment of intense
happiness that they brought to all three of them. And
from the journal to the poems themselves, the ballads and
the touching recollection of 1797 that appears at the end
of *The Prelude* :

> *That summer, under whose indulgent skies*
> *Upon smooth Quantock's airy ridge we roved.*

Here, at any rate, is something that has changed very
little in 150 years. As you drop down from the crest of
the Quantocks (" the turf fading into the mountain road "
still, just as it did when Dorothy noticed it), you first
catch sight of Alfoxden through a screen of trees, standing
in its own little park at the foot of a smooth green slope :
beyond it, a couple of miles away, the sea, which Dorothy
was so often at pains to try and describe. The house is,

in externals at least, almost exactly as it was then, a good gentleman's house of the mid-eighteenth century. Here, looking down on it from above, thinking of the people it once knew and the words they have left behind, one is nearer perhaps than anywhere else to the heart of Georgian Somerset.

It was a brilliant day in April: at that mid-point in the spring when the plum blossom is out, the lilac already in bud, and the daffodils not quite over. We had come across to Wells from Taunton, spending half the morning on the journey, changing at Highbridge and again at Glastonbury; and at length, towards eleven o'clock, we clattered up to Wells in a train that had come straight out of Trollope. For the moment, time had run backwards; we were approaching Barchester in the sixties.

We walked slowly round the town and the cathedral; and last of all, well on in the afternoon, we went into the cloisters. They are, as I had remembered, a little disappointing architecturally—certainly they have not the finished perfection that is the mark of nearly everything else at Wells. One wishes that the parallelogram had been a square; that the ends of the cloisters fitted the doors leading into the cathedral; that the vaulting had all been executed by the hand that made the west walk, for the design of much of the east walk can only be called perfunctory. And yet, for all their formal defects, these cloisters have an intense fascination of their own, from the monuments they contain.

They are none of them ancient. The medieval, Elizabethan, and Jacobean memorials are all in the cathedral itself. It is true that the cloister garth was the burial-place of the canons in the Middle Ages; but no trace of their

graves is now left. The oldest of these monuments dates
back no further than to Charles II's reign : most of them
are Georgian or Regency. They were moved out here
from the aisles of the cathedral at the first restoration a
century ago. If it had not been that several of them commemorated members of families still prominent then in
Wells and the county, they might easily have been destroyed
altogether. The Victorians hated such things. Busy themselves with putting up monuments of their own that are,
with a few exceptions, very greatly inferior in design, they
waged ceaseless war all over the country against the works
of the preceding generations. Even a Late Victorian as
independent and sensitive as Percy Dearmer remarks of
these monuments at Wells that they have been " shifted
to the cloisters, whence, it may be hoped, they will one
day make a further journey towards oblivion ".[1]

But what a narrow judgment that is ! For here on
these walls are the memorials of two centuries of life in
this little town. And they touch wider things too—
literature, music, philosophy, politics, war. The stories
they tell, the way they tell them, the very design of the
monuments themselves, reflect, in their quiet way, something of the whole history of England.

The earliest of them is Bishop Creyghton's, who died
in 1672. Creyghton was a Scot, a Stuart on his mother's
side, and so, as he proudly claimed, a distant relative of the
King's. At Cambridge he was a friend of George Herbert,
whom he succeeded as Public Orator. As a Royalist, he
suffered severely in the Civil War : when Oxford was
taken he escaped to Cornwall, disguised as a labourer, and
so made his way overseas. For fourteen years he was in
exile, sharing the poverty, the humiliations, and the
squabbles of Charles II's *émigré* court. Then, with the

[1] P. Dearmer, *The Cathedral Church of Wells* (1899), 18.

Restoration, his good luck returned. He was at once made Dean of Wells, and in 1670, at the age of seventy-seven, he became Bishop. He has left his mark on the cathedral to this day, for it was he who presented the magnificent brass lectern in the nave, together with the great Bible that stands on it, and most of the sixteenth and seventeenth-century glass in the great west window was also given by him. You can see him lying in marble in the north-east transept. This tablet in the cloisters has been divorced from the tomb to which it belongs.

Not far away, at the south-west corner, there is a fine pair of monuments to a later bishop and his wife : George Hooper, who died in 1727. Like Creyghton, he went to Westminster, and his head master, the formidable Busby, is is said to have remarked of him that " he was the best scholar, the finest gentleman, and will make the completest bishop that ever was educated at Westminster school." The prophecy hardly proved extravagant, for he was one of the most admirable bishops who have ever occupied the see, a notable scholar, and a sensible ecclesiastical statesman besides.

But these two monuments deserve close attention on their own account as well. Both of them are London work, signed by S. Tufnell, of Westminster, of whom very little is known. They are excellent of their kind, sound in design and proportion—though that goes almost without saying for eighteenth-century monuments : even a village mason had an eye for proportion then that his modern successors seem to lack. And one touch lifts Mrs. Hooper's monument high above the conventional. At the top are the three mourning cherubs who are common form in early eighteenth-century work. But here the treatment of the heads is imaginative and living. Each is in a different pose, and the one on the right is an enchanting creature, his little snub nose damaged, his cheeks distended with childish grief. The man who could carve those heads, and group them so perfectly with the swirling wings behind, was a sculptor of real merit.

By intention, too, these monuments are a study in colour. The various marbles used in eighteenth-century memorials were chosen with great care so as to blend satisfactorily, to set off the inscription and the ornaments by a subtle scheme of contrast. At least five different marbles have been used in the bishop's monument, and four in its companion—greys and pinks and yellows and a soft white. But they have deteriorated so much through neglect that it is hard to appreciate this point, impossible to recapture the original colour scheme. These marbles were not meant to be exposed to the air, as they are in the cloisters : no doubt that has had a bad effect on them, and they could never now be brought back to their first condition. But a great deal could be done, and it would be well worth doing. It needs no expensive equipment or elaborate, slow technique, like that required for the restoration of so much medieval work : three-quarters of the task could be carried out with pails of water, cloths and soap. Then, if some of the inscriptions were re-cut and the missing or damaged ornaments restored, these cloister walls would become a gallery of minor eighteenth-century sculpture. Any one who doubts the value of such work should go to Gloucester and study the monuments in the nave, especially the delicate patina of the white and cream marbles, which have taken on just the quality of old ivory through careful washing and polishing. Inside Wells Cathedral everything is so beautifully kept : could not the Dean and Chapter turn their attention to the cloisters too ?

Most of these monuments naturally commemorate people connected with the cathedral, bishops and deans and canons and their wives: Walker King, for instance, friend of Burke and editor of his works; and Catharine, relict of the Right Honourable and Reverend Lord Francis Seymour, Dean of Wells, who in 1801 " put off the trappings of mortality in the assured hope of more perfect bliss ". (The eighteenth-century never lacked assurance, indeed.) But a good deal of the secular public life of the city and county is reflected here, too, in monuments to Members of Parliament and other important citizens like Dr. Claver Morris, the leading physician in Wells under George I, who is known to us because he kept a diary; and John Phelips of Montacute, High Sheriff of Somerset and Chairman of Quarter Sessions, " a station which he continued to fill until acute disease suddenly stopped his career of usefulness on the 20th of April, 1834, at the premature age of fifty years ". There he is, sitting in his chair as Chantrey saw him, type of the earnest intellectuals of his time, with a grave overhanging brow and a calm, slightly troubled expression of face.

Almost beside him, as it happens, are tablets recalling two men of his own generation who fell in the Napoleonic wars: Captain Andrew Foster, a native of Wells, who was killed at the head of the grenadiers of his regiment at the storming of Capetown in 1806; and Charles Edward Foster, a lieutenant in the 1st Dragoons, son of a prebendary and priest-vicar of the cathedral. The inscription here— surely it was written by his father?—is touching in its simple pride: " During the war in Spain he was engaged in various actions with the French, and his gallantry is recorded in the ' Dispatches ' of the Great General under whom he served. Subsequently he accompanied his regiment to Belgium, and fell mortally wounded on the Field of Waterloo, 18th June, 1815, in the 26th year of his age."

But the most interesting of all these monuments stands

away on the other side, in the east walk, close by the entrance to the destroyed Lady Chapel. It commemorates Thomas Linley and two of his talented daughters, Mary Tickell and Elizabeth, Sheridan's first wife. Thomas Linley himself was the son of a carpenter at Wells, where he was born in 1732. He became a musician and set up at Bath as a singing-master. Here he had remarkable success, especially in producing Handel's works at the Assembly Rooms, with his daughters in the leading parts. Elizabeth in particular had a voice of exceptional beauty, but at the age of eighteen, on her marriage to Sheridan, she gave up singing professionally. Instead, she devoted herself to forwarding her husband's political and literary career, until at thirty-eight she developed consumption and died at Bristol. It was a severe blow to Sheridan. As long as she lived she did something to check his intemperance : after her death his life grew rapidly wilder and more extravagant. As for her father, it was one more in a long series of personal griefs. His brilliant son Thomas (Mozart's friend) had been drowned in Lincolnshire in 1778—he never fully recovered from the shock of that news. An extraordinary ill-fortune seemed to haunt his family : of his twelve children, nine had already gone when he himself died in 1795. He was buried at Wells with Mary and Elizabeth and her infant daughter. One monument serves for them all, with an inscription written by his son William. The pedestrian verses still have their faded charm :

> ... *And oh ! my Sisters, peaceful be your Rest*
> *Once more reposing on a Father's breast,*
> *You whom he lov'd, whose notes so soft, so clear,*
> *Would sometimes wildly float upon his Ear,*
> *As the soft Lyre he touch'd with mournful grace*
> *And recollection's tear bedew'd his face. ...*

It calls back the funeral of Elizabeth Sheridan, one of the great occasions in the quiet modern history of Wells. The whole scene is deeply characteristic of the eighteenth century—it comes straight out of Rowlandson. The *cortège* wound slowly over from Bristol, taking a whole day on the journey and arriving between seven and eight o'clock in the evening, watched by a great throng of people. As it advanced up the nave of the cathedral, the bystanders' chattering and movement almost drowned the voice of the priest, and when they reached the vault he was nearly pushed into it. After the funeral was over Sheridan himself returned to the cathedral alone, watching by the grave till midnight in an agony of sorrow. He soon recovered and married again—mistakenly, and as most people thought with indecent speed. But they were wrong if they supposed that his grief for Elizabeth was not genuine. Few people have ever lived more intensely in the moment than he ; and at Wells on that summer night of 1792 his heart seemed broken.

Sheridan, Mozart, Handel, Wellington, Burke—so these memorials and their associations took us back into the eighteenth century. As we emerged from the cloisters into the bright sunshine, walked past the bishop's palace and looked up at the cathedral through the lime trees, the movement of the years seemed to have stopped altogether. And even when we came out into the square, by the town hall and the little shops in all the bustle of a Saturday, time did not move far forward. We knew we were in Barchester still.

# A DEVONSHIRE PARSON OF THE
SEVENTEENTH CENTURY

It is one of the historian's pleasures that he is for ever making new friends—or at any rate new acquaintances. Constantly in the course of his work he comes upon some man or woman who stands out at once as a distinct, a recognisable personality : as distinct, as plainly different from other people, as the men and women he knows in his own life. It may not be anybody important. Very often it is not : some minor figure suddenly shoots out of the written page to stand before him in the full sharpness of reality. It is a startling experience, and it can be disconcerting, for the brilliant life of this one man is apt to put his background out of focus, to make all his surroundings seem unreal : like scenery of canvas and plywood with a human actor in front of it.

Almost at random, I recall one or two of these people who have shown me their obstinate vitality. There is Henry Newman, for instance, Secretary of the S.P.C.K. from 1708 to 1743.[1] His vast, orderly correspondence has survived, and from it we know just what he was like. An exquisitely courteous man—as you can see from the conclusion of this letter, offering to take back into his service a £10-a-year clerk who had left him : " You know the nature of my business and way of life and if you can

---

[1] See W. K. Lowther Clarke, *Eighteenth Century Piety* (1945), chapters ii and iii.

submit to these and promise never to desert me so abruptly as you did I can bear with the defect of your writing in hopes you will take pains to improve it." But here, on the other hand, is his way of dealing with the Governor of Jamaica's chaplain, when he sends over a long-winded sermon to be published by the S.P.C.K. : " Pray how can you afford in respect to your health and your hearers to make such long sermons in a hot country ; if you commonly practise it, it must be a great prejudice to your health if not disgusting to your auditors." How could one better put a pretentious ass in his place ?

So Newman's life passed, given up to the service of the Society and to the sensible, practical philanthropy of his age. He never married : as he remarked when he was fifty-seven, " the Charity Children throughout the Kingdom and my canary birds with my cat and her kitten at home supply the place of children as they engross so much of my time to take care of them ". Indeed he had become an old pussy-cat himself by the time he died, at the age of seventy-three.

Or again, here is the Royalist Sir John Oglander, of Nunwell in the Isle of Wight : a grave, conscientious, upright gentleman who followed the cause of Charles I with immovable devotion. He is a minor figure in Clarendon brought to life before our eyes. For he differed from hundreds of his contemporaries in one thing only, that he was articulate ; and so, when they are forgotten, he lives for us still. " Wouldst thou fain see me, being dead so many years since ? " he asks abruptly, with an uncanny glance at the far future—at us. " I will give thee my own character. Conceive thou sawest an aged, somewhat corpulent man, of middle stature, with a white beard and somewhat big moustaches, riding in black or some sad-coloured clothes over the downs to take the air, morning and evening, and to see there his fatting cattle, on a handsome middling black horse, his hair grey and his complexion very sanguine. Such I conceive myself, and so mayest thou too, if thou hast any desire."[1]

It was seven years ago, in Duke Humphrey's Library at Oxford, that I first made the acquaintance of Edmund Elys. (How many memorable meetings of this kind must have taken place at those desks, under that rich, heraldic roof!) I was working through some of the West-Country papers in Archbishop Sancroft's enormous correspondence, when I came upon this group of letters from an unknown clergyman. The catalogue told me he was rector of East Allington, Devon, from 1659 to 1689. Very soon I learnt a great deal more about him than that.

He was an indefatigable, an incorrigible writer. Letters poured forth from him—and quite a large number of them have been preserved, by the methodical Sancroft and others; he wrote a great deal of cumbrous and indifferent poetry; and he delighted in publishing contentious pamphlets, attacking everything he disapproved of, from " Mr. Cowley's lascivious and profane verses " to cock-fighting. His own words reveal him with a deadly, unforgettable clarity. There he is—cantankerous, self-opinionated, absurd, always in trouble; but appealing in his *naïveté*, and genuinely pathetic : above all a character, and a rich one.

He had a good enough start in life. His father was a former Fellow of Balliol and held the comfortable living of East Allington, behind Kingsbridge; his mother was a Carew of Haccombe, and at Haccombe he was born about 1634. He was sent to the grammar school at Exeter, under William Hayter.[2] Thence, following his father, he

---

[1] Quoted in C. Aspinall-Oglander, *Nunwell Symphony* (1945), 119.
[2] Bodl. MS. Wood F 41, fol. 209. All the MSS. referred to below are in the Bodleian.

went up to Balliol, where he matriculated as a commoner
in 1651. Four years later he too became a Fellow of the
College. He has been spoken of as a " rigid Puritan " at
this time ;[1] but there seems to be no evidence for this
statement, and some to the contrary. It is possible, though
not certain, that on proceeding to his degree he was
required to take the Engagement (the successor to the
Solemn League and Covenant) ;[2] but on his own showing
his previous conduct had been anything but Puritanical.
This is how he described it afterwards, with some relish :
" As in *Hot* and *Sun-shine* Dayes, *Swine* are wont to *Wallow*
in the *Mire* to Avoid the extremity of the *Heat* : So how
long did I accustome my selfe to *Wallow* in all manner of
*Uncleannesse*, (*Filthinesse of the Flesh, and Spirit*) wherein I
never found any True Comfort, did only for the present
Allay the *Scorching* Heat, and Violence of my inordinate
Affections ; being continually Troubled either with the
*Sollicitation* and *Urgency* of them, or with some *Reflexion*
upon the Base and filthy Wayes I tooke to *Satisfie* them ?
. . . The oftener I Accomplisht my Desires, the more
*Discontented* I found My selfe, still *Vexing* My *Spirit*, to
Please My Lusts. But Now, How Happy am I ! Now
GOD is my *Portion* : And what can I Desire more, having
Him who is *All in All* ? "[3]

Many years later, he confessed his undergraduate mis-
demeanours to Archbishop Sancroft in simpler and more
precise terms : " I was guilty of many Indiscretions, and
of some *Gross Sins*, as Fighting in the Schooles, Vainglorious Disputing, Excessive Drinking &c."[4]

[1] H. W. C. Davis, *Balliol College* (1899), 140.
[2] Sir Charles Mallet, *History of the University of Oxford* (1924-1927), ii. 386.
[3] *The Quiet Soule* (1659), 4-5. I have preserved Elys's orthography throughout,
since it is characteristic of the man, only expanding some contractions and
occasionally altering his punctuation. His dates may be taken to be in the Old
Style.
[4] Elys to Sancroft, 6 April 1678 : MS. Tanner 314, fol. 43.

It is to be feared that "vainglorious disputing" remained one of Elys's characteristics long after he had cast off his other vices. Moreover, he was already a confirmed scribbler : he was hardly of age before he published his first pamphlet, and from then onwards the stream was incessant. Much of what he wrote in these early years was in verse, but this practice was evidently frowned upon in some quarters—particularly by Bishop Gauden of Exeter[1]—and he soon abandoned it. "I never Publisht any Verses", he told the Archbishop in 1680, "that doe not as to their Subiect become my Function except some Epigrams and near 20 years since I did in Print *Recant* the Printing of them. And yet they were as Innocent as any Verses of such a nature ever were, and accompany'd with many Serious Verses."[2]

In 1659 he was imprisoned at Exeter as a suspected Royalist ; but on his father's death in the same year he quietly succeeded him as Rector of East Allington. He was presented to the living by Edmund Fortescue of Fallapit, who may perhaps have been his pupil at Oxford, since he matriculated at Balliol in August 1658.[3] Elys's pamphlet on cock-fighting, which came out in 1660, was dedicated to him and Dennis Granville, afterwards Dean of Durham, as "my most dearly beloved and honoured Friends."[4] Fortescue was Elys's patron—a most eligible one in the early years of Charles II's reign, for he was created a baronet in 1664 and became M.P. for Plympton in October 1666. But before that year was out he was dead, at the age of twenty-three, and soon afterwards the fortunes of his *protégé* began to decline also. Not immediately, for a year or two later he was well enough off to

---

[1] Elys to Sancroft, 26 March 1678 : MS. Tanner 39, fol. 15.
[2] Elys to Sancroft 2 January 1680 : MS. Tanner 37, fol. 223.
[3] Wood, *Athenae Oxonienses*, ed. Bliss, iv. 470 ; Foster, *Al. Oxon.*
[4] The pamphlet was reprinted in the *Harleian Miscellany* (1744 ed.), vi. 110-15.

P.E.                                                                   F

send a handsome donation to a fund that had been raised
for discharging the debts of his old College ;[1] but in the
course of the next ten years he went steadily downhill.

When Archbishop Sheldon died in 1677, he was succeeded by William Sancroft, Dean of St. Paul's. Elys was
in London (staying " at the Surgeon's Arms in Bruges
Street in Covent Garden ") just after the new Archbishop's
consecration, and he took the opportunity to write to him,
explaining his misfortunes at length and begging him for
some preferment. His living, he said, was worth £130-140
a year. But out of that sum he paid an allowance of £24
towards the maintenance of his mother, two brothers,
and a sister : he had " a vast Load of Debts " and not as
much as £40 a year on which to keep himself and his wife
—" though I could well bestow above £50 yearly in
Books ". He complained of the inhumanity of his creditors :
there were also, he said, people owing money to him,
which they would not pay.[2] Two months later he followed
this up with a direct request to Sancroft for a loan of
£20.[3]

Elys seems now to have taken up his residence in
London, keeping a curate to look after the parish of East
Allington. His affairs went from bad to worse, and on
2 January 1680 he found himself in the King's Bench
prison.[4] Thence, a year later, he wrote to Sancroft again,
imploring his help. His parishioners, it seems, were refusing
to pay him their dues without a law-suit (which, he candidly
adds, " I confess I am very unfit to manage "). He was
being disgracefully slandered, especially by those who said
he suffered from " *a certain unsettleness* of mind. As to
that I boldly Aver that I have Cause to suppose that there

---

[1] Davis, op. cit., 141.
[2] Elys to Sancroft, 28 January 1677 : MS. Tanner 314, fol. 9.
[3] Elys to Sancroft, 26 March 1678 : MS. Tanner 39, fol. 15.
[4] Elys to Sancroft, 26 May 1680 : MS. Tanner 37, fol. 36.

is not any person living that has from his Youth been
more Averse then my selfe from being Addicted to any
*loose Variable* Opinions in Theologie." He hastened to
defend himself also against another charge that had been
brought against him, in a wistful sentence with a paragraph
all to itself: " I very seldome make Verses now in any
Language ". The heady, exciting days of his youth were
indeed long past. He ends up his letter with a pathetically
humble appeal to the Archbishop for anything he may
think fit to send, " tho' but the sum of a few shillings ".[1]

It is evident that Sancroft—who was rich and gave his
money away freely—now came to the rescue, for a few
days later Elys wrote to thank him for what he had sent.
His wife, he said, joined him in gratitude. She had been
with him all through his troubles.[2] Poor woman! She
must have had a great deal to put up with. She was well
connected herself—a niece of Lord Berkeley of Stratton;
and she had brought her husband a substantial dowry. But
she can never have known much comfort after her marriage,
and she died at no great age in 1684.[3] As a widower, Elys
was now touchingly forlorn. " I have an Averseness from
all Company ", he wrote, " except in Case of *Necessity* in
respect of *Christian Civility,* and Visiting the Sick, and
other Business. . . . This Summer I have often frequented
a *Solitary House* by the Sea-side on a Rock near a village
that was lately swallow'd up in the Sea."[4] But even this
retirement—harmless and easily understandable, one would
have thought—was made the cause of gossip by his enemies:
they could hardly have cried out against him more, he
complained, if he had turned foot-pad.

[1] Elys to Sancroft, 2 January 1680: MS. Tanner 37, fol. 223.
[2] Elys to Sancroft, 8 January 1680: MS. Tanner 37, fol. 231.
[3] Elys to Sancroft, 9 September 1684: MS. Tanner 32, fol. 136.
[4] Elys to Dennis Granville, 17 December 1684: MS. Rawlinson D 851, fol. 267.

Yet however much one may sympathise with Elys in his misfortunes, one can see how irritating, how tactless he was. The last letter was written to his old friend Dennis Granville, its ostensible purpose to congratulate him on his appointment to the deanery of Durham. It was a rich deanery; and Elys could not forgo the opportunity of asking for a loan. At the same time he showed himself anxious to resume regular correspondence with Granville, which had apparently lapsed. It would be enough, he said, if Granville wrote two or three times a year; but he himself would write much more often. " I shall not expect long letters from you," he wound up grimly, " tho' you will seldome receive short ones from me." Three weeks later he returned to the chase with a deplorable poem written in praise of the Dean's sister, Lady Joanna Thornhill. The " *Poetick Instinct* " came to him, it seems, on New Year's Day. He composed the verses in Latin when he woke up in the morning, went to sleep again, and then wrote them down before he got out of bed. Next day he translated them into English. The Dean was at liberty to show them to his sister or to suppress them. One wonders what[1] Dean Granville—that delightful, worldly-wise prelate— thought of this. Did he administer a crushing rebuke to the poor rector of East Allington, or did he just tear up his letters as they arrived? At all events, no more of them have been preserved among his papers.

Up to this point, Elys's troubles had been mainly financial. Henceforward, they were political. The reign of James II was a difficult time for Anglicans, whether they were time-servers or conscientious churchmen. Elys, according to his lights, was undoubtedly in the second class. He went so far towards passive obedience as to read the King's notorious Declaration of Indulgence at least

---

[1] Elys to Granville, 8 January, 1684: MS. Rawlinson d 851, fol. 270.

once in his church in May 1688. He was hotly attacked for this action and flew, as usual, to paper and print for his defence, which appeared in a broadsheet entitled *A Clergyman of the Church of England His Vindication of Himself for Reading His Majesties Late Declaration.*[1] This account of his proceedings, disentangled from the jargon in which he involved it, has a two-fold interest. First, it shows clearly enough the sort of problem a country clergyman might be faced with in this matter through the nature of the Declaration itself and through the delays and inefficiency of seventeenth-century episcopal administration. Elys states that he read the Declaration under the belief that it had been sent to him by the Bishop of Exeter : it was not until nearly another week had elapsed that he received an intimation that the Bishop did not wish him to read it. And secondly, it throws light on the attitude of that particular bishop, Thomas Lamplugh. He was an altogether more supple spirit, and he found himself between the upper and the nether millstone ; for while he was anxious to please the King, he also wanted to stand well with his fellow-bishops. It must have been an alarming moment for him when he heard that Sancroft, the Archbishop of Canterbury, had taken the lead in refusing to promulgate the Declaration, and that among the rest of the Seven Bishops were his two neighbours, Ken of Bath and Wells and Trelawny of Bristol (who was his personal enemy and coveted his see).[2]

No such difficult questions of high politics troubled Elys, who was simple-minded and muddle-headed, but certainly not venal. That he was indeed disinterested he proved a year later when the real test came : he then refused to take the oaths of allegiance to William III and Mary,

---

[1] There is a copy of this broadsheet in the Bodleian : Ashmole G 12 (134a).
[2] On this point cf. *Devon and Cornwall Notes and Queries*, xxii. 168.

who had supplanted James II, and so became a Non-Juror. Here he was once more in the same camp as Sancroft, to whom he wrote a letter setting forth his reasons for declining the oaths. "For me to be *Turn'd out of my Parsonage*", he says, "(in this Parsonage-House I would rather Live than in any other House in England) will be, in the sight of Men, a very Tragical thing."[1] But it happened; and Elys retired from East Allington to Totnes, where he seems to have lived for the rest of his life. His passion for pamphleteering continued unabated. He now made onslaughts on Locke's *Letter Concerning Toleration* (which he characterised as " the most Devillish piece of Sophistrie that I ever saw ") and the *Essay Concerning Human Understanding*, so following up an attack he had made in 1681 on another political classic of his time, Hobbes' *Leviathan*. He also presented to his fellow Non-Juror Thomas Smith " as a Token of my Peculiar Affection about a sheet and halfe in Latine with this Title JOANNIS MILTONI Sententiae Potestatis REGIAE Adversantis Refutatio ".[2]

Against almost all Nonconformists he waged incessant warfare. He fought Baxter, Ludlow, and John Owen in pamphlets, and he carried on a furious vendetta with a local enemy, John Flavel, a Dissenter of Dartmouth. On the other hand—this is one of the surprising things about him—he praised and defended the Quakers, at a time when very few Anglicans had a good word to say for them. He was also an admirer of Henry More, the Cambridge Platonist, whose *Letters on Several Subjects* he edited and published in 1694.

We have few details of his declining years, apart from those his pamphlets provide, and what we have come

[1] Elys to Sancroft, 5 June 1689: MS. Tanner 27, fol. 38.
[2] Elys to Smith, n.d., and 26 September 1690 (MS. Smith 49, ff. 203, 217); MS. Rawlinson J 4to. 4, fol. 182.

mainly from the antiquaries. Knowing of Anthony Wood's labours on the *Athenae Oxonienses*, he wrote to offer him details of his friends' careers. His first letter is thus endorsed in Wood's sturdy scholar's hand : " Edm. Elys sometimes of Ball. Coll. now Minr. of Totnes ; who by his study, or something else, has brought himself into a crazed condition. This letter I received on Christmas Day but did not answer it, because I knew so much of the writer, that whatsoever had passed between us, he would have made public."[1] However, it appears that Wood did write to him a year later, and in reply Elys sent a number of details about the lives of his Devonshire contemporaries, which were diligently noted.[2]

Another distinguished antiquary, White Kennett (then archdeacon of Huntingdon and afterwards bishop of Peterborough), also heard from Elys. In 1702 he was shown a printed *Letter to Dr. Kennett* concerning the great Convocation controversy then raging, signed " Your Servant in the Love of all Truth and Justice Edmund Ellys ". Kennett then remembered that he had received the *Letter* from Totnes about eighteen months before ; but " I neglected an answer because indeed I thought the writer *non compos* of it ".[3]

Poor Elys ! He must by this time have become very eccentric. We catch one further glimpse of him, tormented by asthma and still living at Totnes, from the second edition of *The Quiet Soule*, published at Exeter in 1707, and then he vanishes altogether. One cannot doubt he went on scribbling to the last.

[1] MS. Wood F 41, fol. 189.
[2] ibid., ff. 191-210.
[3] MS. Ballard 7, fol. 109.

THE CITY of Exeter has been besieged six times since the Norman Conquest. The last and the longest of these sieges occurred in the great Civil War, in which it played a vital part : it was, indeed, the central pivot on which the whole of the fighting in the West Country turned.

When the War began, the allegiance of the citizens was divided. It is symbolic that of the two Members Exeter returned to the House of Commons in November 1640, one became a Royalist, while the other was a staunch Parliamentarian. Most of the townspeople took the side of the Parliament. That was only to be expected. It was what happened all over the country : almost everywhere the middle classes in the towns were against the King. And here there was special reason, besides, why this should be so ; for the Russells, Earls of Bedford, were the most powerful family in the city, and they too were Parliamentarians. On the other hand, there was also a strong element of Royalist feeling in Exeter. The influence of the Church was on the King's side, and as in all cathedral cities the lead given by the dean and chapter was important. Even the corporation was not wholly of one mind : it included some Royalist members, who consistently voted against the Puritan majority.

For the moment, however, the supporters of the Parliament had it all their own way. In August 1642 the

King dispatched the Marquess of Hertford and the Earl of Bath to raise the West for him; but Exeter shut its gates against them, and the corporation sent a polite message, refusing to admit the Earl into the city. That autumn the war began in earnest. In January 1643 Parliament appointed as its commander-in-chief in Devon and Cornwall the Earl of Stamford. It was a double mistake. Stamford's main asset was that he was a peer and exceedingly wealthy. But he was irritable, cantankerous, self-important; and—just as serious—he was a complete stranger to the West Country. He was a Leicestershire Grey himself, quite unfitted to understand the tenacious local patriotism of Devon and Cornwall. He made his headquarters in Exeter; but he had hardly arrived before the tide began to turn against his cause in the West. In Cornwall, where Royalist feeling was very much stronger than it was in Devonshire, the King's troops won their first considerable success at Braddock Down, between Liskeard and Lostwithiel, on 19 January. Four months afterwards came a much greater victory at Stratton, won for the King against odds, in position and in numbers, by the Cornish infantry under Sir Bevil Grenville.

The effects of the battle were immediate. The whole of Devonshire fell at once into the King's hands, excepting only five towns : Exeter, Dartmouth, Plymouth, Bideford, and Barnstaple. The Royalists had already made one attempt to surprise Exeter, in the previous winter. Now they began a more formidable, systematic investment. The Earl of Warwick, who was commander-in-chief of the navy, was instructed by Parliament to try and relieve the city from the sea, and in July he sailed up the river to Topsham, whence the guns of his ships could command the flat country and cover a landing; but the Royalists were prepared to receive him, and after three or four hours' firing he was obliged to retreat on the ebb tide with two of his ships captured and one burnt.

Inside the city, preparations for its defence were made at high speed and with small regard to expense. Over £18,000 was spent by the citizens on the work in the first eight months of 1643. Half that sum went to the soldiers in pay.[1] The fortifications ate up a great deal of the rest. The city accounts show us how the money was expended: on carrying stone and felling trees; on tools and shovels and wheelbarrows; on work at the Exe bridge, at Rougemont castle and the city gates, at Northernhay and Southernhay, at "the fryers and the Maudlyn" (how long the medieval memories lingered!); £300 to Mr. Robins for seventeen packs of wool taken from his cellars to reinforce the batteries. It is all set out and accounted for with meticulous care: total £4,374 11s. 3½d.[2]

Late in August the King's young nephew Prince Maurice arrived to take command of the siege, and little more than a fortnight afterwards the city surrendered to him, on 4 September 1643. Sir John Berkeley, who had taken a leading part in the whole operation, was now made governor of Exeter. His appointment was welcomed by Robert Herrick, who was then living in his Devonshire vicarage of Dean Prior, in an elegant, courtly poem:

> *Stand forth, brave man, since Fate has made thee here*
> *The Hector over aged Exeter ;*
> *Who for a long sad time has weeping stood,*
> *Like a poor lady lost in widowhood :*
> *But fears not now to see her safety sold*
> *(As other towns and cities were) for gold,*

---

[1] W. Cotton and H. Woollcombe, *Gleanings from the Municipal and Cathedral Records . . . of the City of Exeter* (1877), 90.
[2] Historical MSS. Commission: *Report on the Records of the City of Exeter* (1916), 208.

*By those ignoble births, which shame the stem*
*That gave progermination unto them :*
*Whose restless ghosts shall hear their children sing,*
*" Our sires betrayed their country and their king "* . . .

That praise was well deserved, for Berkeley was an upright
and honourable soldier, who would never have betrayed
his trust.

Exeter was now the headquarters of the King's army
and administration in the West Country, a base as important
to him as Oxford and Chester. A mint was established in
the city. Presently it became a royal residence. In the
spring of 1644 the Queen was pregnant. It seemed unwise
for her to give birth to her child in Oxford, where she and
Charles were then living, for Oxford was almost in the
front line of the war ; and so Exeter was chosen for her
confinement instead. She stayed in Bedford House, the
great ramshackle mansion of the Earls of Bedford. (It
was pulled down in 1780, to be replaced by the splendid
Bedford Circus that the Germans have now destroyed.)
There she gave birth to a daughter on 16 June : the
Princess Henrietta, her fifth child. The Queen herself
was especially obnoxious to the Puritans, for she was a
Catholic and a Frenchwoman, suspected—not at all unjustly
—of being the King's evil genius. The House of Commons
had voted her impeachment, and she was no longer safe
in England. Accordingly, less than a month after her
delivery, she left Exeter for Falmouth, where she took ship
over to France.

The baby stayed behind ; and at a month old she was
christened in Exeter cathedral, with Sir John Berkeley as
godfather. A golden bowl was used for the purpose—
not the marble font that still stands in the south aisle of the
nave, with the great round bowl, the cherubs' heads, and

the slender, pure white stem : that was added to the cathedral forty years afterwards, in 1684. It is touching to think of what happened to the child baptised there on that summer day. She became Charles II's favourite sister ; at seventeen she was married to the Duke of Orleans, a jealous husband ; she shone at the French and English courts, and was one of the patrons of Molière and Racine ; in 1670 she was sent on a secret political mission from Louis XIV to her brother and died immediately afterwards, aged twenty-six ; Bossuet delivered one of the greatest of all his sermons at her funeral. So much sprang from the birth of that child at Exeter in June 1644.

The next royal visitors to the city were the King and the Prince of Wales. Charles I came twice, staying in Bedford House and knighting the mayor, Hugh Crocker, on his arrival. Both his visits were brief interludes on the way to and from his victorious campaign in Cornwall. That was the St. Martin's summer of his success. The following year, 1645, brought him disastrous defeat at Naseby and then, in September, the loss of Bristol, which laid the whole West Country open to Fairfax and the advancing Parliamentary army. Once again Exeter was directly threatened with a siege.

Inside the city, tempers were changing. Where at the beginning of the war there had been a good deal of enthusiasm on one side or the other, on the part of many of the more substantial citizens at least, now we can detect little but weariness, a longing for the fighting to end. Here, as elsewhere, it was largely a matter of the cost. At the outset money had been forthcoming freely—nearly £4,500 in plate and cash in 1643.[1] But when this easily-realised capital had been spent, money could be found only with a great deal more difficulty, and the continual demands for

---

[1] Cotton and Woollcombe, op. cit., 90.

contributions, levied for one purpose and another, produced increasing irritation and decreasing returns. £300 had been raised, without a murmur, for presents to Lord Stamford at the opening of the war.[1] A further £500 was bestowed on Prince Maurice and Sir John Berkeley soon after their entrance into the city.[2] But when the Prince of Wales came down in August 1645, a present of £100 had to be made to him and, " there being no other means to raise the same ", the disgraceful expedient was adopted of plundering a charity. For that year—and one may guess for some time afterwards—the orphans of Exeter had to go short.[3]

And now Fairfax was outside, plainly determined to reduce the city once and for all. The plan he adopted for taking the city was closely similar to that of William the Conqueror when he invested Exeter in 1068. It was to plant a series of strong points outside, until the city was ringed round with his forts : completely cut off from the rest of the world, it could then be hammered and starved into surrender. Fairfax began on the east. He made his headquarters at Silverton, sending a scouting party across to the Yeo valley and another to the south to secure Topsham : he then determined to place garrisons at Nutwell, Bishop's Clyst, Poltimore, and Stoke Canon. You can see very clearly what his idea was from the map, or better still from walking up the shallow, rich Clyst valley and crossing over to the Exe by Poltimore and Huxham. In spite of the railways and the pylons and the airfield, the structure of the country has not changed. There, to your left all the time, is the hill on which Exeter stands— a great peninsula humped up between the two rivers. It was Fairfax's object to isolate it.

[1] ibid., 86.
[2] ibid., 93.
[3] ibid., 103.

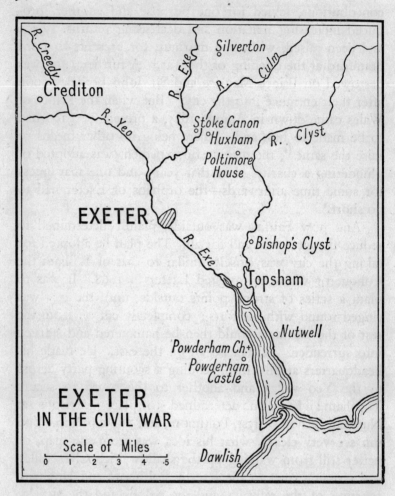

The garrisons east of the Exe were completed by the end of November. Now it was time to begin work on the west. One of the most important points on that side was Powderham castle, which was held by the Royalists. It had been a standing annoyance to the Parliamentarian party in Exeter since the beginning of the war: they had been anxious to capture, and if possible demolish, it as early as 1643.[1] Fairfax now determined to try and surprise it without delay. We have a full account of this exciting little operation, written by a chaplain in the Parliamentary army.[2] On Sunday night, 14 December (the weather was fiercely cold), two hundred men were sent across the Exe from Nutwell. They found that the garrison of the castle had just been reinforced, and it was too strong for them to take ; but they seized and fortified the church instead, hard down by the shore. There they were attacked the following night by the Royalists, who kept up a strong assault with hand grenades for three hours. But all to no purpose. The little garrison held firm, and the attackers, we are told, " were beaten off with much loss, leaving their dead on the place, and carrying with them many wounded, as appeared by the snow, that was much stained with their blood as they retreated ". In spite of this success, however, the position of the men in the church was grim, for they were wholly without fuel in the black winter weather. Clearly the place could not be held ; but they would not leave it until they were expressly commanded to by Fairfax. (This was the spirit and discipline that made the New Model army invincible.) Two days later their orders came, and they were safely withdrawn across the river.

As you travel down in the train from Exeter to Dawlish and Plymouth, you pass very close to the little red Powderham church, with its dark avenue of ilexes. Think sometimes, when you see it as you pass by, of the fighting there in those December nights of 1645.

Though this assault on Powderham failed, the castle had only a short reprieve : six weeks later it fell

---

[1] ibid., 87.
[2] Joshua Sprigg, *Anglia Rediviva* (1854 ed.), 171-3.

into the Parliament's hands. Exeter was now completely surrounded by Fairfax's chain of posts. In February he won his victory at Torrington : early in March he was able to pin down the last Royalist army in Cornwall and force its surrender. Then he felt strong enough to turn back to Exeter to bring the siege to a close. On 31 March he summoned it to capitulate. " There is nothing more induceth me hereunto," he wrote in his letter to Berkeley, " than an unfeigned zeal toward any bloodshed, and, as much as in me lies, to preserve that city, which hath already suffered deeply in these unnatural distractions, from further or greater misery " ; and these words were sincere, for Fairfax was a deeply humane soldier.

The garrison's position was now hopeless. It could not look for relief, since the King had no army left in the field ; the city had already been damaged by enemy attack —homeless refugees were even finding shelter in the ruined bishop's palace ; here, as everywhere else, there was a great weariness of the war ; and a majority of the influential townspeople were in any case Parliamentarians, in sympathy with the besiegers. Berkeley therefore agreed to treat.

The negotiations, which were carried through in Poltimore House, resulted in extremely favourable terms for the Royalists. The defenders were to march out of Exeter with the full honours of war ; there were to be reasonable guarantees of the Royalists' personal safety ; the corporate privileges of the city were not to be interfered with or diminished. Altogether, it was a generous, moderate settlement ; and on Monday, 13 April, the garrison marched away " by twelve of the clock at noon, with their horses, full arms, bag and baggage, and their goods, colours flying, drums beating, matches lighted." The last of Exeter's sieges had been brought to an honourable end.

WHO WROTE the first English guide-book ? It is a difficult question to answer. But the guide-book as we know it may be said to emerge—like so very much else—in the seventeenth century. It started as, quite literally, a *guide book* : a book, that is, that should act as a guide, a signpost, to the roads the traveller followed. Here is the title of one of the earliest, published in 1635 : *A direction for the English traveller, by which he shall be enabled to coast about all England and Wales, and also to know how far any market-town lieth from another.* A little later on, in Charles II's reign, the guide-book began to acquire maps ; and in the eighteenth century the information in the text was expanded. Besides a bare table of distances, it would give particulars of the towns that were to be seen on the way, and especially of the houses : the name of the owner, some historical information (it might or might not be accurate), an occasional titbit of gossip. Now here are all the essential elements of the modern guide-book : directions for finding your way, maps to make that easier, instructions about the things to see on your journey and what to look for when you arrive.

The demand for guide-books grew much greater in the late eighteenth century, for a number of clear reasons : the improvement of the roads, which made it so much easier and pleasanter to travel ; the development of watering-

places, Bath and Buxton and Brighton; the new feeling
for landscape—the rustic, the picturesque, the romantic,
the horrid. And then on top of this came a fresh interest
in history (promoted most of all by the novels of Scott),
in architecture, in natural science. The guide-book now
became more serious. It was no longer enough for it to
point out a gentleman's seat and record an anecdote about
a ghost that was reputed to appear there : the reader
wanted much more than that, and he began to get it.

Take an early West-Country guide-book as an example :
Octavian Blewitt's *Panorama of Torquay*—the second edition,
greatly enlarged, was published in 1832. It begins with a
description of the scenery of Torbay and then passes quickly
on to a section called " Outlines of Geology ", followed
by others on history, climate, statistics, botany, and so on.
Mr. Blewitt was a doctor of a literary turn of mind, and
no expert in the scientific and historical parts of his work ;
but he had the good sense to quote freely from recognised
authorities, and the botanical section was contributed by
a learned lady, Miss Griffiths. The writer of a guide-book,
then as now, had to be omniscient. Failing that, then as
now, he had to fall back on the knowledge of other people,
and his skill consisted in blending as much reliable information as he could in the most palatable and convenient form.

It was in 1851—the year of the Great Exhibition, of
*The Stones of Venice* and Turner's death—that the first of
a new series of guide-books appeared : *A Hand-Book for
Travellers in Devon and Cornwall*, published by John Murray
at six shillings. Notice, by the way, that the first of them
*was* the *Devon and Cornwall* : a publisher always likes to
launch a series with a volume that he thinks will sell, and
the West Country had already attained its modern popularity
with tourists. Besides, a journey into Cornwall then was
a real adventure : it was like going abroad. None of the

main railways was yet open. You either drove down by
the old road through Launceston or you put your carriage
and horses on the "steam bridge" that crossed the
Hamoaze by Plymouth. (The Torpoint ferry, that venerable
institution, has changed little in the past hundred years.)

Murray's *Handbooks* ultimately covered the whole of
Great Britain and most of the civilised world ; and on the
whole they must be reckoned the best of all our guide-
books—clear, accurate, wide-ranging, constantly infor-
mative companions on any journey. One of them, Thorne's
*Environs of London*, is a masterpiece ; and several of the
county *Handbooks*—the *Lincolnshire*, for instance, and the
*Warwickshire*—are almost as good.

I said they were "wide-ranging". By that I meant
that they did not confine themselves to one kind of information, scientific or antiquarian, and that they showed a
close interest in the present as well as in the past. Look at
the section on "Mines" in the *Devon and Cornwall* of 1851.
First comes an admirable account of their early history, of
the Phoenicians, the Romans, the medieval Stannaries ;
then we consider mechanisation and modern processes of
mining ; and from that we pass naturally to instructions
on going down a mine :

"The traveller who is desirous of descending a mine
must lay aside every article of his ordinary dress and array
himself in the costume of a miner—a flannel shirt and
trowsers, worn close to the skin in order to absorb the
perspiration, a strong pair of shoes, a linen cap, and a stout
broad-brimmed hat, intended to serve the purpose of a
helmet in warding off blows from the rock. He then has
a candle fixed to his hat by a lump of clay, and is equipped
for the adventure. . . .

"The most interesting mines for the traveller to descend
are those near the Land's End, which penetrate beneath the

sea ; for in these, when the coast is lashed by a swell from the Atlantic, an accompaniment that is seldom wanting, he may hear in the levels the harsh grating of rocks rolling to and fro overhead in the bed of the sea, and the reverberation of the breaking waves ; but the enjoyment of such sublime but portentous sounds will require strength of nerve in the visitor, as the noise is often so terrific as to scare the miners from their work."

What could be clearer, more sensible, or more exciting to one's curiosity ?

Murray's *Handbooks* did really try to furnish useful information about all sides of the life and work of the English counties. That is what gives them their clear supremacy among our guide-books. They were followed, as the nineteenth century went on, by other series and by innumerable single volumes, large and small, endlessly entertaining for the curious (and often useless) information they afford.

Their advertisements alone are enchanting. How they take one back into that remote Victorian world, so sedate and secure, so earnest in the pursuit of high-minded pleasure ! Here is a shop at Lynmouth that sells wools and pipes and newspapers, Epps' Homœopathic Medicines, and —last of all, a final draw if all else fails—Fern Trowels and Baskets. Or we are at Weston in the seventies, and Mr. Griffith the chemist is anxious that we should buy his Essence of Sea-Weed, for spinal affections, lumbago, tumours, weakness of the limbs, scrofula, etc. We go to Penzance, and there is Mr. Drew on the Esplanade, who runs " the very first Manufactory for converting Cornish Serpentine into cheap, useful, and Ornamental Articles, among which are Exquisite Thermometers, . . . Obelisks, Hebe Jugs, . . . Fonts, Chalices (Antique and Modern) ", and a score of other things. Would he have a ready sale now, I wonder, for " One Hundred Minerals, scientifically arranged in a Case, with descriptive catalogue, from £1 to £3 " ? I doubt it : our minds have moved so far away from the Victorians', our pleasures are so much more frivolous than theirs.

But what an infinite debt we owe them for their industry, their patience, their unremitting attention to the serious business of life ! Here, as everywhere else : for it was the stores of learning they amassed that made possible a new, and much more scientific, treatment of local history. It was they who built up those antiquarian societies whose work has contributed so much to English provincial life. In the West Country the oldest of them is pre-Victorian : the Royal Institution of Cornwall, which was founded in 1819. The Somersetshire Archaeological and Natural History Society celebrated its centenary at Taunton in June 1949 ; the Devonshire Association dates from 1862 ; and so on. All these societies did invaluable work in promoting the study of local history. And gradually their collective learning began to be absorbed into the guide-books.

It was not a quick process. The *Transactions* and *Proceedings* of these societies went on appearing quietly for a long time, making an appeal only to the cultured circle of their members. But at the end of the century a new series of guide-books was started that did take some account of the work that had been published there. These were the " Little Guides ", the first volume of which was issued by Methuen in the autumn of 1900.

I think it is interesting to contrast the " Little Guides " with the Murray's *Handbooks* that had preceded them. Physically they had some great advantages : they were smaller—books genuinely made for the pocket—and more attractive to look at, better printed, better bound, supplied with a much better map. And they were illustrated, with drawings and photographs, whereas no " Murray " ever contained a picture.

The text, too, was quite different. It was arranged on another plan, for one thing. Instead of taking the traveller on a series of journeys through the county and telling him what to look out for on his way—the old method, as we have seen, reaching back into the seventeenth century—these " Little Guides " gave their account of each parish in alphabetical order. But what was most important of all was their different emphasis. The " Little Guides " were almost wholly concerned with antiquities. They did not share the keen interest in contemporary life that was expressed in Murray's *Handbooks*. It was not entirely excluded from them, but it took a minor place in their scheme. Two-thirds of the new guides were devoted straight away to the churches, so that in parish after parish the reader gets the impression that nothing but the church is worth looking at : houses, farm-buildings, bridges, roads, let alone social customs and peculiarities—they are all subordinated to the churches. And then, finally, the taste of the books, naturally and pardonably, reflected the taste of the age they were written in. To their authors, Gothic architecture was the height of human achievement : the Renaissance and classical work that followed it nothing but a disappointment, a degradation.

The first of the " Little Guides " to be published for a western county was the *Cornwall* of 1903. It was followed by *Hampshire, Dorset, Devon, Somerset, Wiltshire,* in that order ; and the set was rounded off by *Gloucestershire,* which appeared in the spring of 1914. They varied very much in quality : that was only to be expected. The best of them, I think, was the *Dorset* : the worst, beyond question, the *Cornwall,* a miserable farrago of gossip and mistakes. But let us look for a moment at the *Devon*, which seems to me the most remarkable *book* of them all.

It was written by Baring-Gould, and it has his personality stamped all over it : dictatorial and summary in judgment, at once shallow, slapdash, and learned, full of curious anecdote—above all the work of a living man, who cared passionately for the country he was writing about. It could have been written by nobody else, and even the shortest shelf of Devon books must include it.

But guide-books go out of date very quickly, unless their authors revise them every few years with meticulous care. The " Little Guides " were revised, but seldom carefully, and not always by their authors. Mistakes of the most obvious sort went on being repeated in edition after edition. To give a single example. Baring-Gould, in his careless way, stated that John Ford, the Devonshire dramatist, was born in 1505 and died in 1639. Now turn to the ninth edition of the book, published in 1931 after a " considerable revision " by Mr. R. L. P. Jowitt and a complete re-setting of the text, which presumably meant that somebody read the proofs : believe it or not, John Ford is still stated to have died at the impossible age of 134 ! If a blunder like that can go on appearing, it is unlikely that more serious errors will be corrected : neither will the book be brought truly up to date.

Now at last a complete revision of the " Little Guides " has been taken in hand, and all those covering the West Country have been re-issued in a new format.[1] The pictures are better, though well below the high standard they ought to reach nowadays : they are reproduced on poor paper,

---

[1] *Cornwall* : by Arthur L. Salmon, revised by H. Ronald Hicks. *Devonshire* : by S. Baring-Gould, revised by H. Ronald Hicks. *Dorset* : by Frank R. Heath, revised by E. T. Long. *Gloucestershire* : by J. Charles Cox, revised by H. Stratton Davis. *Hampshire* : by J. Charles Cox, revised by R. L. P. Jowitt. *Somerset* : by G. W. and J. H. Wade, revised by Maxwell Fraser. *Wiltshire* : by Frank R. Heath, revised by R. L. P. Jowitt. (Methuen and Batsford. 1949-1950.)

in the gruesome sepia colour beloved by Messrs. Batsford, and by nobody else. But what about the text, which matters much more? Once again, it is a story of very varied achievement. The new *Dorset* comes out brilliantly. Mr. Heath's original book was very good. The revision, by Mr. E. T. Long, is even better. Here is a really careful guide, scholarly, unhurried, well proportioned: I am tempted to say it is as good as Murray's *Lincolnshire*, and I can hardly give it higher praise.

But, alas, they do not all reach that level. The *Somerset* was never a good book: it skated through that wonderfully rich county in impatient haste. It has now been somewhat improved, but all kinds of shortcomings remain. The account of Bruton is full of inaccuracies; Prior Park, the most important Georgian house in the county, is dismissed in twenty words; the large wall-painting of St. Christopher in the church at Wedmore is still not mentioned; at Ilchester we hear nothing of Sheridan or the famous gaol; Mr. T. S. Eliot is not referred to under " East Coker ", though most visitors will know its name only from his poem.

The *Devonshire* is even more disappointing: a slapdash revision of a slapdash book. A number of errors have been corrected, it is true; but others have arrived in their place, and a good deal of the wayward, inconsequent charm of Baring-Gould has been removed. Some of the new mistakes are astounding. Mr. Hicks, the reviser, seems to have no natural sense of chronology at all, and his reference to the Monk family under " Great Torrington " is one of the most absurd things I have ever found in a guide-book —which is saying a good deal: he manages to make George Monk (who restored Charles II to the throne in 1660) the father of Admiral Byng, who was shot for the loss of Minorca nearly a hundred years later. One can

hardly take the book seriously after that. No : I prefer
the old Baring-Gould, with all his faults—just as I prefer
an unrestored church to one that has been " improved "
by a tasteless and ignorant rebuilding.

The new *Cornwall* is even worse. In revising the book,
Mr. Hicks had a rotten foundation to build upon ; but I
fear it cannot even be said that he has made the best of a
bad job. Apart from mistakes—and there are plenty of
them—the omissions in the book are egregious. The
parishes of St. Ewe and Lanreath, for example, are not
described at all. Yet the church of St. Ewe has one of the
most remarkable of West-Country screens, with a cornice
as good as any in Devon, and the Grylls monument at
Lanreath is of exceptional interest. But then neither the
original author nor the reviser knows much about churches.
The peculiar features of Cornish church architecture are
passed over without mention. All we get, time after time,
is the uninformative comment that the style of the church
is " Perp.". As if that helped. The implication—quite
false—is that all " Perp." is the same. One does much
better with an old Victorian book like J. T. Blight's
*Churches of West Cornwall.* It was last printed in 1885 ;
but it is more useful than the " Little Guide " of 1950.

It is essential, to my mind, that the compiler of a guide-
book should show a catholic taste. He ought surely to
mention everything worth seeing, whether he personally
likes or dislikes it ; for his first business is not to praise or
condemn, but to tell the traveller what to look out for,
leaving him to make his own judgments. If you agree
with that view, this *Cornwall* will certainly not please you.
It displays the usual romantic approach to the county, the
usual failure to understand its astonishing modern industrial
development. Tin-mines and china-clay workings are
referred to only as eyesores. The section on " mining "

in the introduction is laughable. It gives us five paragraphs on the industry from the Bronze Age to the Romans and then jumps on at once to describe its depression in the 1920s : not a word of the nineteenth century, when it was of European importance.

Here again one cannot help feeling that the Victorians were saner and kept a better balance. Murray's *Handbook* of 1851 is still, from many points of view, the most profitable guide-book to use in Devon and Cornwall in 1951. There is no reason why it should not be superseded, if some one will set himself to the task who is intelligent, accurate, sensible, and discerning. Then at last we shall get a guide-book that really meets the needs of the modern traveller. For my own part, I shall welcome it most warmly when it comes. But I reserve the right to go on, even then, carrying my old " Murray " and a few other Victorian guides about with me. For there are not many books that take one's mind back so swiftly and surely into the world of the 1850s : when Palmerston represented Tiverton and Rajah Brooke was living under Dartmoor ; when Thomas Hardy was a pupil-architect in Dorchester ; when Mr. Hewett, showing Exeter to visitors, could tell them that they would find " the neighbourhood abounding on every side with quiet rural walks, field paths, and ' Devonshire lanes ', each displaying its peculiar charming and diversified scenery, and often leading to a quiet tea or ' junket ' house ".

IT IS just over two hundred years since Johnson published his great poem *The Vanity of Human Wishes*. There is a famous passage in it that describes the danger and misery of the life of learning. It has all the force of Johnson's own experience behind it :

> *Deign on the passing world to turn thine eyes*
> *And pause awhile from letters to be wise ;*
> *There mark what ills the scholar's life assail,*
> *Toil, envy, want, the patron, and the jail.*
> *See nations slowly wise, and meanly just,*
> *To buried merit raise the tardy bust.*
> *If dreams yet flatter, once again attend,*
> *Hear Lydiat's life, and Galileo's end.*

Every one knows something of Galileo, of his death in the prison of the Inquisition at Rome. But who was Lydiat ? And why should Johnson have picked out his life to stand as such a dreadful warning ? The commentators are not very helpful. They give us the outline of Lydiat's career, but they hardly explain Johnson's interest in him. To understand that one must go further, back into the memories and the gossip of Oxford two hundred and fifty years ago.

Thomas Lydiat was born at Alkerton in north Oxford-

shire in 1572.[1]  He came, we may infer, of a family of
well-to-do yeomen : his father owned the patronage of
the living of Alkerton, but he is described in the entry of
his son's matriculation at Oxford as " pleb.[2]"    Thomas
went to Winchester and then, at the age of nineteen, to
New College, where he quickly made his mark as a scholar.
He suffered from some imperfection of speech and from
a defective memory—or was that merely the familiar absent-
mindedness of the learned ?  Apparently for these reasons,
he gave up the study of divinity, the prelude to a promising
career in the church, resigned his college fellowship in
1603, and devoted himself wholly to mathematics.    His
special field was the study of chronology, and he threw
himself into it with immense ardour, publishing four
books on it in the years 1605-1609.  He became involved
in an abusive controversy with the great Scaliger, from
which he emerged with credit.   In 1609 he was appointed
chronologer and cosmographer to Henry, Prince of Wales.
The title of his office was more imposing than its salary,
40 marks (or £26 13s. 4d.) a year.  But it brought him
into personal touch with Prince Henry and the circle of
rising and able men who were gathering round him.

In the same year he met James Usher, then Professor
of Divinity in the new Trinity College, Dublin.  Usher too
was deep in chronological studies.   He was at once
interested in Lydiat and bore him off on a long visit to
Ireland.  While he was there, Lydiat became incorporated
at Trinity and held an appointment as reader in the College.
Shortly afterwards he stood for the mastership of Armagh
school.  He seems to have wanted the post earnestly, and
Usher was able to exercise valuable influence on his behalf,

[1] The fullest account of him is in Anthony Wood, *Athenae Oxonienses*, ed.
P. Bliss (1813-1820), iii. 185-8.
[2] *Register of the University of Oxford*, ed. C. W. Boase and A. Clark (1885-1889),
vol. ii, part 2, p. 187.

for the Archbishop of Armagh was his uncle.[1]  But
for some reason or other, Lydiat failed to secure the
place.

A worse blow fell on him in the next year, 1612. Prince
Henry died. It was the occasion for one of those outbursts
of formal elegy that make the poets of the seventeenth
century so agreeably absurd to us. But some of those who
mourned the Prince felt his death in the most personal
sense. Whether they had really loved him or not, they had
looked to him as the future king, the most desirable of all
patrons after his father, whose promises—to men of letters,
at any rate—were thought to be larger than his performance.
The Prince's death broke up the circle that had centred
on him. Like the other members of it, Lydiat had suddenly
to fend for himself. At once he took a false, a fatal
step. When his father, some years before, had offered to
present him to the rectory of Alkerton, he had refused it.
Now his father was dead, but the presentation remained in
his family. The opportunity was there, through a vacancy
in the living. He reconsidered the matter and reversed his
earlier decision. In 1612 he returned to his birth-place as
Rector.

It probably seemed a wise thing to do at the time, in
a moment of crisis, and we should beware of writing
Lydiat down as a simple-minded fool, in the light of our
knowledge of what subsequently happened. For some
years things seem to have gone fairly well with him. He
continued his research—he was, after all, only a long day's
ride out of Oxford : a further instalment of his controversy
with Scaliger appeared in 1613, two works on the solar
year in 1620, another on the Golden Number in 1621. He
still corresponded with Usher.[2] He was sufficiently well

---

[1] R. Parr, *Life of . . . James Usher* (1686) : *Collection of three hundred Letters* appended
to the work, 13, 15.
[2] ibid., 39, 43, 57, 68.

off to begin the building of a new parsonage at Alkerton, which survives to this day. The parish register records the laying of its foundation-stone on 2 May 1625.[1] But his prosperity did not last much longer. On 13 February 1627 he found himself in the King's Bench prison in London.[2] He was never out of trouble for the rest of his life.

It appears that he had been unwise enough to go security for debts incurred by his brother, and that his brother had let him down. When he made the mistake of returning to Alkerton his family seem to have taken the opportunity to fleece him. It is a common story, though here it has an unusual pathos : the ageing, unworldly scholar, interested only in his research and preyed upon by his relations. He remained in prison, intermittently if not continuously, for a number of years, until he was in the end extricated through the good offices and financial help of Laud and Usher (who is said to have spent £300 on him) and Warden Pink of New College.[3] He then petitioned Charles I for a permit to travel abroad to the Near East and Abyssinia in search of manuscripts. It is a pity his request was not granted, for that would have put him well beyond the reach of his family. It might also have kept him out of the troubles that caused his death.

As it was, however, he returned to Alkerton. We know little of his life there in the 1630s, but one grim silence proves that it cannot have been happy : he published not a single book after 1621. Not that his work had stopped. When he was in prison, so the traditional story ran, " he was observed to be cheerful, and to carry on his studies with the utmost diligence, being so entirely addicted

---

[1] *Parochial Collections for Oxfordshire*, ed. F. N. Davis (Oxfordshire Record Society, 1920), 5-6.

[2] The date may be calculated from a sentence in a letter from Lydiat to Patrick Young in the Bodleian : MS. Bodley 670, fol. 20.

[3] Thomas Hearne, *Remarks and Collections* (1885-1921), i. 297.

to them that he laid out what money he got upon books, so that he was in a manner starved to death : which made Dr. Potter,[1] when he sent him a benevolence of £5, give him a strict charge to spend none of it in books, but take care to get what might recruit his macerated body ".[2]

We can see so well what kind of man he was : guileless, unpractical, unworldly. If we needed any further proof of that, we should find it in his conduct on the outbreak of the Civil War. Most people, with seventy years of such a life behind them, would have had enough and been anxious only to keep out of trouble, in the manner of the Vicar of Bray. But not Lydiat. When the war began he at once made clear his sympathy with the King. He lived in an awkward place for a Royalist, uncomfortably near the Puritan town of Banbury, only four or five miles from the battlefield of Edge Hill. His house was looted by Parliamentarian troops, he was hustled off to prison twice, and at last he died at his rectory in April 1646.

That is the story as it has generally been told. It is dismal enough, but is it quite so terrible as to put it in the same class as Galileo's ? If you look through Walker's *Sufferings of the Clergy*, the Royalist account of the persecution of the Anglican Church during the Civil War and the Interregnum, you will find other tales of equal hardship. Why, again, should Johnson have singled out Lydiat for that special mention ?

The clue to the answer lies, I believe, in a manuscript at the Bodleian. There a nameless writer records the tradition that Lydiat was " plundered by the soldiers of the Parliament, where endeavouring to defend his books

[1] Hannibal Potter, President of Trinity College, Oxford.
[2] Hearne, op. cit., i. 197.

in his study, the soldiers broke in, threw him down the stairs, broke his shoulder etc., upon which he died ".[1] That story receives some confirmation from the Latin preface to a work of Lydiat's that was published less than thirty years after his death. The soldiers, so the writer tells us, " overwhelmed him with wounds and blows, and treated him with such barbarity that he died within two days."[2] It certainly looks as if Lydiat, after all his troubles, met a violent end in his old age.

There is no way of telling if those stories are true. They may be fabrications, or embroidery on Lydiat's known misfortunes. But the important thing is that they were recorded. Lydiat's memory lived on, until it merged into the vast mythology of Oxford. That surely is how Johnson heard of him. When he was up at Pembroke in the 1720s, there must still have been old dons about who knew the great Lydiat Legend. It is not difficult to imagine their relish as they passed it round, safe themselves from all trials like his in the calm reign of the Georges.

In any case, the certain story of Lydiat's life is sufficiently grim. It was a disappointing, a wretched career. Only a small proportion of his work was published in his lifetime. Soon after his death some effort was made to collect his papers and print something from them, but it came to nothing. A good many of them disappeared in the havoc at Alkerton rectory. The rest were gathered up by a villager, stuffed into a corn-sack in his cottage, and devoured at leisure by beetles and grubs. From this indignity they were rescued by John Lamphire, the Oxford doctor who later attended Anthony Wood.[3] Now at least they were valued, and Lamphire had them bound up in twenty-two volumes. But their troubles were not

[1] Bodlian Library: MS. Rawlinson B. 158, fol. 146.
[2] Preface to Lydiat's *Canones Chronologici* (1675).
[3] ibid.

over even then. In the spring of 1659 he had a fire at his house and a number of them were destroyed. In the end only one was published : *Canones Chronologici*, which came out in 1675. The rest remain still in manuscript at the Bodleian, and it is unlikely now that they will ever find a printer.

A little of Lydiat's work did, however, live on. For Usher—who was a greater man, tougher, richer, and a good deal more lucky—continued with his chronological studies, incorporating work in which Lydiat had helped him. He brought them to a point in two volumes of *Annales* (published in 1650 and 1654), translated into English and published in 1658 as *The Annals of the World . . . to the Beginning of the Emperor Vespasian's Reign*. On this book was based the chronology of the Old and New Testaments that was accepted by the Anglican Church without question until the nineteenth century. The dates assigned to events by Usher (the Creation, 4004 B.C. ; the Ark, 2349 ; Exodus, 1491 ; and so on) continued to be printed in the margins of the Bible. I remember them well in a copy that I used as a child : for all I know they may appear in some editions still.

Only one work of Lydiat's can really be said to endure, and that is the house he built : the house that saw his death, whatever that may have been. It was repaired in 1692, and again in our own time, but its external appearance has undergone very little change. It is a pleasant walk out there from Banbury, along by the park of Wroxton, climbing up towards Edge Hill from the back. Suddenly there is a sharp double bend in the road. You are on the edge of a steep little valley, and there at the corner is Alkerton church and the Jacobean rectory, built of the strong golden stone from Hornton, a bare mile away. As you walk on—to Compton Wynyates, or up on to Edge

Hill itself—the figure of Lydiat will lodge itself in your mind.  He was "a person of small stature," Wood tells us, "yet of great parts and of a public soul"; and he is commemorated in a line of poetry for ever.

# PARISH HISTORY

" To THE historian of England between the Revolution
and the Municipal Corporations Act, if he is not to leave
out of account the lives of five-sixths of the population,
the constitutional development of the parish and the
manifold activities of its officers will loom at least as large
as dynastic intrigues, the alternations of Parliamentary
factions, or the complications of foreign politics." So
wrote the Webbs in 1906,[1] and what they said of the
eighteenth century is almost as true of the sixteenth and
seventeenth also. Yet, in spite of its importance, the subject
has been very little studied. We have had some good
histories of separate parishes, and books dealing with
particular aspects of parochial history in general—the poor
law, church rates, tithe, and so on. But no one, since the
Webbs, has been bold enough to attempt a wide view of
the whole great field, even over a limited period.

Plainly the reason lies in the intimidating nature of the
material. There are more than 12,000 parishes in England
and Wales. Life is not long enough to allow any scholar,
or group of scholars, to examine them all. How much
easier, then, to confine yourself to the records of one parish
or a small district or, at the widest, a single county. You
can become intimate with your subject to a degree that is
attainable in hardly any other kind of historical writing:

[1] S. and B. Webb, *English Local Government* . . . : *the Parish and the County* (1924
ed.), 5.

you may even feel, in the end, that you have come near to exhausting all the material that exists.

There is, however, the other kind of local history : the Webbs' kind, a survey on a comparative basis of many different parishes, towns, dioceses, counties. This demands an accurate understanding of local conditions, of the differences between one region and another ; and, rightly handled, it has perhaps more to offer to the general historian.

To this study Mr. W. E. Tate has made a notable contribution. In his book *The Parish Chest*[1] he sets out to answer the question : What does one find in the parish chest ? What documents does it contain, and what is their value ? He has himself investigated a good many of the chests of Nottinghamshire, Staffordshire, and two of the Yorkshire Ridings ; and he has been able to make use of printed surveys of the documents of seven other counties, and of many single parishes elsewhere in England as well. His sample is therefore large enough to be truly representative, though there are counties—Cornwall, for instance —that he scarcely touches on in his survey.

Anybody who has ever examined the contents of a parish chest for himself will know one thing for a start : that you never can tell what may be inside it. Mr. Tate gives us instances of some of the very odd things that have been preserved there—medical prescriptions, wills, warrants for holding a court-martial, the cast of an Elizabethan Plough Monday play at Donington in Lincolnshire. More personal documents are sometimes to be found : the household accounts of two Georgian vicars of Batheaston and their sisters, several clerical diaries. Perhaps I may add two examples of a rather different class from those given by Mr. Tate : the interesting description of the

[1] Cambridge University Press, 1946.

parish of High Ham in Somerset, written by its parson
(a German) in the reign of Elizabeth ;[1] and the running
commentary on the Civil War kept up, partly in cipher,
by the Parliamentarian parish clerk of St. Mary's, Beverley.

The first characteristic of these documents, then, is
their bewildering variety, and this, quite as much as their
total bulk, must hitherto have deterred historians from
making adequate use of them. It is here that Mr. Tate's
book is so valuable, for it provides us with a general
classification of the material. It begins with a brief account
of the parish and then passes on to divide the documents
into two groups : " Records mainly Ecclesiastical " and
" Records mainly Civil ". The first of these sections
includes parish registers, churchwardens' accounts, the
records of parochial charities (always an interesting subject),
of tithes and church courts. The second starts with vestry
minutes, going on to petty constables' accounts, the
records of poor-law and highway administration, of
agriculture, and finally of enclosures—Mr. Tate's special
field.

A bare enumeration of these headings will remind us
of the great sweep of English life that was comprised within
the parish until it gradually lost its powers, swallowed up
in the larger groupings of modern administration. But
the book is more than a mere catalogue or inventory.
Each of these topics is illustrated from Mr. Tate's own
reading and research ; so that if he writes primarily for
professional students of history, he has also a great deal to
say to any one who is interested in English country life.
Here is a single example, two sentences in which, as he
truly says, " the authentic voice of rural England speaks ".
An effort was made in 1709 to settle some German refugees

---

[1] See *Proceedings of the Somersetshire Archaeological Society*, vol. xl (1894), part 2,
pages 113-22.

from the Palatinate as labourers in Kent. With this result at Cowden : "Where as A Vesterey Has Bin called By The Churchwardens & overseares of the Parish of Cowden. We Hoose names are Heare Under subscribed Chiefs of The in Habitance of the Parish of Cowden Have no occashun for any of the Pallatins, for wee Have more of ouer one Poor than we can imploy, nither Have we any Housing to Pott them in."[1]

Most attractive of all—and rare in work of the kind—this book distinctly reveals something of the personality of its author. Mr. Tate is not afraid of comment or, where he feels strongly, of expressing his own opinions (though very many of his readers will disagree with them). In his preface he remarks that " if this book is soon superseded by a better, its author will be delighted ". That is altogether too modest. It will be supplemented, and at some points corrected ; but it will be a long time before it is replaced. For many years to come it is likely to remain the standard introduction to an important, and neglected, mass of historical material.

Mr. Tate's book is an example of what I have called the " comparative " study of parish history. The other method—the study of the history of one parish in and for itself—has been very much more commonly used, and it is a great deal older. Parish history can boast at least one classic from the seventeenth century : White Kennett's *Parochial Antiquities attempted in the History of Ambrosden, Burcester, and other adjacent Parts in the Counties of Oxford and Bucks,* first published in 1695 and re-edited (how many other parish histories have deserved such an attention ?) by Dr. Bandinel, Bodley's Librarian, in 1818. Kennett's book has a severely practical origin, like so much of our historical writing in this country. He was presented to the

[1] Tate, op. cit., 164.

living of Ambrosden in 1685 and when he arrived there
he found, so he tells us, " some disturbance in the parish
about the manner of expending and accounting for the
annual profits of certain lands and tenements allotted to
*pious uses* ". On referring to his bishop and to the patron
of the living, he was advised to investigate the history of
the parochial charities. That autumn he got a sight of
some papers in the church chest and made an abstract of
them, though he tells us that he managed this only " with
some difficulty ".[1] Clearly some one had something to
hide : I do not think it would be unjust to suspect it was
one of the churchwardens.

So Kennett's inquiries began, and like many other
students he found the work grew under his hand. What
started as an investigation of a parochial scandal soon
became one of the whole history of the parish of Ambrosden and its neighbours. " When I had once begun to be
thus inquisitive," he says, " the slow discoveries which I
gradually made did not so much satisfy my mind as they
did incite it to more impatient desires. So that diverting
from my ordinary course of studies, I fell to search for
private papers and public evidences, to examine chartularies
and other manuscripts, and by degrees to run over all
printed volumes, which I thought might afford any manner
of knowledge of this parish, and the adjacent parts of the
country."[2] His *Parochial Antiquities* made its appearance as
a stout quarto volume ten years after its author began the
simple inquiries from which it took its rise.

To a modern reader, the book is not entirely satisfactory. For one thing, it is cast in the form of annals, and
they reach down only to the year 1460. Again, the Father
of Parish History shows himself prone to the temptation

[1] *Parochial Antiquities* (1818 ed.), vol. i, p. ix.
[2] ibid., vol. i, p. xiii.

that has beset so many of his descendants : the temptation
to irrelevancy, to disquisitions on general subjects that are
of only indirect importance for the history of the parish.
Here, for instance, under the year 1336 we come upon a
diatribe twenty-five pages long on papal abuses, the
iniquities of the appropriation of churches to monastic
houses, the character of the English Reformation, the
Church history of the seventeenth century.[1] Kennett felt
deeply on these matters—he afterwards wrote a book on
appropriation ; but it is a pity he introduced them here,
where they distort the work and hold up its progress.

Yet when these criticisms have been passed, the book
remains a landmark. Not only because it is, in time, the
first really important history of a parish that we have, but
for its own virtues, which give it a permanent place in
English historical writing. Look at one of the excellent
principles that Kennett states in his preface : " Where I
wanted authorities, I resolved my conjectures should be
short and modest ".[2] He followed it out faithfully in
practice. Would that some of his successors had paid an
equal attention to it ! The book is learned, judicious,
thorough ; and—something that should by no means be
taken for granted—it is clearly and soberly written.

If we now move forward to our own time to see how
the writing of parish history has changed since its foundation in the seventeenth century, we shall find that in some
respects it shows notable development. The sources of
information, it goes without saying, have multiplied. The
public records—national, diocesan, county—are available
for our examination with a freedom and completeness of
which Kennett could never have dreamt. Again, when he
wrote he dismissed prehistory in a terse little chapter of

[1] ibid., ii. 39-65.
[2] ibid., vol. i, p. xiv.

two pages, on the good principle, quoted above, of cutting down conjecture about subjects on which he had no certain information. Today we can do better than that : our knowledge of early history has so immensely increased. Above all, we have come to take a wider and deeper view of the meaning of parish history than our forefathers did. We consider the parish as a society quite as much as an institution. That means that many things that in earlier days would have seemed beneath, or outside, notice are now of the highest interest to us : the lives of the poor, for instance, the cottages that are their outward symbol. White Kennett, indeed, " endeavoured to be very accurate in the descent of families, and the conveyance of estates ".[1] But by " families " he meant only noble and gentle families, together with a few wealthy yeomen. The parish historian today is—or I think he should be—interested in families of all classes : especially, perhaps, in the poor, for our information about their lives in the past is so fragmentary and intermittent.

In scale, our modern works vary greatly. The biggest are not necessarily the best—though there is much to be said for the method adopted by James Parker in editing Samuel Barfield's history of Thatcham in Berkshire. Here a large quarto volume, on the usual lines, is followed by a second, containing the text of all the important documents on which the narrative has been based. That was in 1901, however. With our present costs of printing and paper, we can rarely contemplate following this good precedent. But our modern parish histories can still be admirable, even when they are short. It is difficult to single one out for special mention. I should like to discuss the late Mr. Pearse Chope's *Book of Hartland* (1940), which is one of the best that has ever been written. But Hartland

[1] ibid.

is itself such a remarkable parish, a subject so completely made to the historian's hand, that I prefer to choose as an example one that can lay claim to no special distinction of its own : Galby in Leicestershire, whose history has been written by Dr. W. G. Hoskins.[1]

It is indeed an unexciting place to look at, half a dozen miles out of Leicester to the south-east. It has only one memorable thing to show : a church tower of 1741 with pinnacles of an oddly Chinese appearance. Otherwise it has, on the surface, very little to distinguish it from its neighbours. Here are the same gentle green slopes, the same dull brick buildings, as you find in scores of other East Midland parishes. But Dr. Hoskins—who has studied those scores himself—leads us directly to the things that are of special interest here. He shows us how the lack of a resident squire affected the place ; and how its story is one of a gradual decline from the fifteenth century onwards, arrested for a moment in the seventeenth century, and then continuing unchecked into our own time. The population of Galby today is half what it was in 1670 and little more than a third of the population of 1381.

Galby, then, is an unromantic place now, with a rather melancholy history behind it. Dr. Hoskins considers it with the clear eye of the historian. He does not invest it with any bogus glamour. Yet how full of interest the story is, as he tells it ! Here, for instance, is the old medieval chapel of Frisby, dependent upon Galby. It fell into decay after the Reformation : by the early eighteenth century it had been wholly forgotten. But its site is still known as Chapel Mount, and some of its timbers are in use as gate-posts : one of them supports the roof of a farm-building. " Thus ", as Dr. Hoskins says, " the old

---

[1] Printed in his *Essays in Leicestershire History* (Liverpool University Press, 1950), 24-66.

roof-timbers that were living trees at the time of the Norman Conquest are still doing good work."

"Doing good work": that is what pleases this historian, a craftsman who has a special sympathy for his fellow-craftsmen and loves the things they produced. This comes out most clearly in his discussion of the wills of Galby people in the sixteenth and seventeenth centuries and the inventories of their goods. These inventories form a class of evidence for our social and economic history that has not yet been adequately used, and Dr. Hoskins is himself something of a pioneer in showing us their value.[1] Here we can see, step by step, in Galby the improvements brought about in domestic comfort: new articles of furniture—chairs and cushions and hangings; the addition of an upper floor to the house, making it possible ultimately to remove the beds from the parlour, to separate living and sleeping accommodation altogether.

One could multiply examples of this kind. Dr. Hoskins has so much to tell us of the history of Galby that throws light on the social history of the whole of England. Yet he does not digress from his main theme, as White Kennett did over appropriation. He sticks tenaciously to his subject all the time; but because he is an historian, well versed in the social and economic history of England, he can demonstrate the wider, general significance of the little things that are happening in Galby, whether it is changes in domestic equipment or in agricultural method or in the relationship of social classes.

Parish histories like this one are rare, however, and they will remain so, for they demand skill and knowledge and judgment of a high order. I do not want to suggest that works of this kind alone are valuable. The ordinary short

[1] Cf. his important papers on the Leicestershire country parson and the Leicestershire farmer in the sixteenth century in the same volume of *Essays*.

parish history, compiled by an amateur, can be a useful and delightful book. If I turn now, finally, to discuss one that seems to me unsatisfactory, it is not because I wish to be churlish—still less to attack a particularly bad book, for it is by no means the worst of its kind; but because the faults it displays are so common and so easily remedied.

Twenty miles away from Galby, on the other side of Leicester, lies the parish of Coleorton. It offers a splendid subject to an historian: for it is itself of considerable natural and historic interest, it has a church remarkable for its fittings, and a Hall well known to students of English literature and English art. In fact it is one of those places—like Ashby-de-la-Zouch near by, like Leicester itself—whose history forms part of the history of England.

Yet no one has ever written the history of Coleorton. What an opportunity missed! Look at the range of interest that is to be found in this one place. An important part, to begin with, in our industrial history, for it was the centre of the main production of coal in Elizabethan Leicestershire; and it was a Coleorton man, Huntingdon Beaumont, who seems to have been responsible for the earliest railway of which we have record in England, which appears at Wollaton in Nottinghamshire in 1597.[1] The mention of Huntingdon Beaumont leads us straight to the history of his family, who held the manor of Coleorton for 500 years. No less than eight of them find a place in the *Dictionary of National Biography*: from the great group in the sixteenth century, which included Francis the dramatist, to Sir George Beaumont, who was the friend of Wordsworth and Constable and a principal founder of the National Gallery. And so we come at last to our own time, when—to complete the familiar tale—

[1] J. U. Nef, *The Rise of the British Coal Industry* (1932), ii. 14; C. E. Lee, *The Evolution of Railways* (1937), 14-15.

Coleorton Hall ceases to be the home of the Beaumonts and becomes an office of the National Coal Board instead.

There, then, is a summary of the story that the Rector of Coleorton sets out to tell in a short history of his parish. It is based largely, so he informs us, on material collected by his predecessors, as well as on his own inquiries, and it must be taken as a set of notes rather than as a connected narrative. The notes are discursive, scrappy, and in some places disappointingly meagre. They are discursive because the author does not stick closely to his subject (that spectre irrelevance again!). " Coleorton and the Beaumonts " offers scope for a book many times the size of this one : yet after less than twenty pages we are being conducted away to Ashby and Coalville and Breedon-on-the-Hill. Surprisingly, we then return to Coleorton to look at the church and consider its incumbents : only to wander off again into " Some Notes on the Diocese of Leicester "— a subject that has nothing to do with that of the book. With a little further reading, too, the Rector could easily have amplified his account of Coleorton. He could have told us more, for instance, of the seventeenth-century parsons : of Thomas Pestell, an interesting poet whose works have been republished lately ; of William his son, who had a hard time of it in the Civil War ; and of Samuel Oldershaw, the Puritan " intruder " during the Interregnum.[1] Or again he could have said much more of the friendship between the Wordsworths and Sir George Beaumont if he had supplemented Knight's *Memorials of Coleorton* by Professor de Selincourt's great edition of the Wordsworth correspondence.

The Rector of Coleorton might perhaps reply that his book is intended only to be a sketch, not a full history, and

---

[1] See A. G. Matthews, *Walker Revised* (1948), 241-2, and *Calamy Revised* (1934), 373, with references there cited.

that of course is true. But by merely omitting what does not bear directly on his subject he could have made room for a good deal of interesting matter without increasing the size or the price of his book at all. We may be grateful to him for drawing attention to one of the most remarkable parishes in Leicestershire; but it is impossible not to wish, all the same, that he had taken his inquiries further.

Perhaps, after making this criticism, it may be fair to state what seem to me to be the things to aim at in writing a brief history of a parish. First of all, a sound acquaintance with the printed material that is available. An exhaustive study of all the original documents would be beyond the scope of a pamphlet such as this, and appropriate only to a section in the *Victoria County History* or to a substantial book. A great mass of material for the history of any English parish is accessible, however, in print. Much of it is local—county histories, newspapers, the *Transactions* and *Proceedings* of county archaeological societies. But there is in addition a good deal to be gleaned from works of national scope, which are to be seen in the larger libraries : the *Dictionary of National Biography*, the *Complete Peerage*, the *Calendars of State Papers*, the *Reports* of the Historical Manuscripts Commission, and so on. The work of consulting them is apt to be laborious, but the effort is well worth making, for it will often yield material of great importance. Then, when all the likely sources of printed material have been examined, it is desirable to go one stage further : to supplement the parish documents (which may be good or bad, exciting or almost useless) by others in the County Record Office and the local ecclesiastical archives—particularly rewarding in Leicestershire, since the records of the archdeaconry are unusually interesting, and well preserved in the Muniment Room of the City Museum.

So much for the written material. But there is a great deal more that is valuable : local traditions and memories (such as the Rector's delightful picture of Miss Merewether playing the seraphine in Coleorton church a hundred years ago) ; the fabrics of the old buildings—farm-houses and cottages as well as church and hall ; the fields and woods and water of the place itself. They are all part of the evidence for the long human occupation of the site that the historian is trying first to unravel and then to piece together into a continuous narrative. Where it happens, as at Coleorton, that a great family has lived in the place, the story should be all the more interesting ; for they have usually left strong traces of themselves behind them, in letters, in portraits, sometimes in the very furniture and books they used, transmitted carefully down to their descendants.

Here are the real materials of local history : the story of life lived in one place for a thousand or two thousand years. And the local historian's purpose should surely be to tell that story as clearly as he can ; fully, yet tersely ; and with all the concentration he can command, looking straight at his subject and neither to right nor left. With these aims in mind his story will begin to tell itself ; and what could be more fascinating than the true story of a parish in England ?

# A LEICESTER ARCHITECT
## 1732-1814

IN THE past two hundred and fifty years Leicester has produced a surprising number of interesting architects. There is the obscure figure of Sir William Wilson (1641-1710), who designed the new nave, transepts, and tower of St. Mary's church at Warwick when they were rebuilt after the fire of 1694, and collaborated with Wren in the astonishing Grammar School at Appleby Parva : he is said to have been the son of a Leicester baker.[1] There are the Wings, father and son : the father, who rebuilt the nave and tower of Galby church in 1741 ; the son, who was the architect of the beautiful church of King's Norton in 1770.[2] Moving on a century, we come to F. W. Ordish, a forgotten genius of the Gothic Revival.

But there is another Leicester architect whose work is perhaps known more widely : John Johnson, who designed the Shire Hall at Chelmsford and the County Rooms in his native town. In this paper I wish to gather up what I have been able to find out about his life and works. I am not competent to deal with them from a technical point of view : my prime purpose is biographical, not critical.

Johnson was born on 22 April 1732 and baptised in

---

[1] *Publications of the Wren Society*, xi. 85, 108-13 ; and T. Edwards in *Country Life*, 7 July 1950, pp. 44-5.
[2] J. Throsby, *Supplementary Volume to the Leicestershire Views* (1790), 137-8 ; *Transactions of the Leics. Archaeological Society*, xxii. 179-80, 193.

THE SHIRE HALL, CHELMSFORD (1791)
From an engraving by I. P. Malcolm in John Johnson's
*Plans, Sections and Perspective Elevation of the
Shire Hall, Chelmsford* (1808)

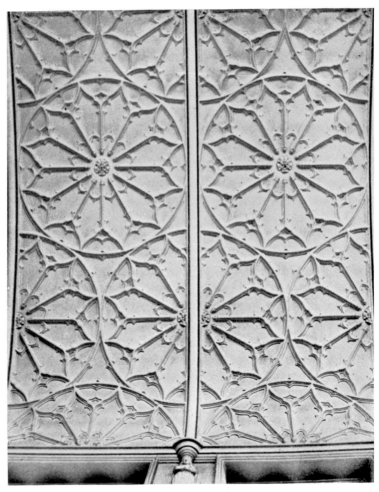

ROOF OF THE NAVE, ST. MARY'S CHURCH
(NOW THE CATHEDRAL), CHELMSFORD

St. Martin's church on the following 23 July.[1] His father was John Johnson (1707 ?-1780), and his mother's name was Frances. I have been able to recover nothing certain about either of them. The name " John Johnson " is, of course, a common one, and it occurs many times in the Freeman's Register; but of the eighteenth-century John Johnsons who are recorded there none can easily be identified with the architect's father, and I am inclined to think he was never a freeman of the borough.

John was born in Southgate Street.[2] We know nothing of his early career—unless he was the John Johnson, eldest son of John, joiner, who was admitted a freeman on 22 April 1754.[3] At the time of his death it was stated that " he left this town . . . in early life possessing little more than strong natural abilities, which soon found their way in the Metropolis ".[4] With that unsatisfying statement we must be content. It would be most interesting to know how he gained his instruction and experience as an architect: for he emerges quite suddenly, with a wide practice, at the age of fifty. None of the buildings he is known to have designed can, so far as I am aware, be dated earlier than 1782.

In the spring of that year he was appointed Surveyor to the County of Essex.[5] His residence was then given as Berners Street in the parish of St. Marylebone, and he continued to live in that parish until shortly before his death. His predecessor, William Hillyer, had just died in office, and it is possible that Johnson had been acting in some way as his assistant, since one account is signed by him in the year 1781.[6]

[1] St. Martin's parish register.
[2] Nichols, *History of Leicestershire*, i. 528.
[3] H. Hartopp (ed.), *Register of the Freemen of Leicester* (1927), i. 315.
[4] Obituary notice : *Leicester Journal*, 16 September 1814.
[5] His appointment was made at the Epiphany Quarter Sessions : Essex Record Office, Q/SO. 13, page 263.
[6] Essex Record Office, Q/FAC, 5/1.

P.E.                                                                               I

The office to which he was appointed was officially designated " Surveyor of the Gaol, Houses of Correction, Bridges, and other Buildings in and belonging to this County ".[1] That compendiously describes the main part of the Surveyor's official work : he combined what we should now call the posts of County Surveyor and County Architect. He seems to have been paid chiefly by fees for the preparation of plans and a commission of 5 per cent. on the cost of all works that he supervised.[2] No doubt he also received some retaining fee, but I have not been able to discover its amount. The Surveyor is to be regarded rather as a standing consultant than as a full-time servant of the county. Johnson continued to live in London and went down to Essex when it was necessary. I cannot find any evidence that he had a house in Chelmsford : his name does not appear, for example, in the rate-books, nor among those of the residents in the parish who were assessed for the rebuilding of the church from 1800 onwards.[3] Throughout the time of his service as the Essex Surveyor he maintained a substantial private practice as an architect. That was usual in Johnson's time, and for long afterwards. To take a somewhat later example from Leicester : William Parsons designed the new gaol in Welford Road (which was completed in 1828) as part of his official duties as County Surveyor ; but he was also the architect of St. George's church.[4] It is convenient to examine Johnson's work under two headings : first his official work in Essex and second his commissions elsewhere.

At the time of his appointment in 1781 a new county

---

[1] Essex Record Office, Q/SO. 13, page 263.
[2] E.g. for his work on the House of Correction at Halstead : Essex Record Office, Q/FAC. 5/1.
[3] Chelmsford churchwardens' accounts.
[4] J. Curtis, *Topographical History of the County of Leicester* (1831), 111.

gaol had lately been finished at Chelmsford, to Hillyer's designs. It stood on the south bank of the river immediately beyond Moulsham Bridge, on the right-hand side of the road. John Howard had visited it in 1779, and had given it his general approval ;[1] but it was already in need of alteration and extension, and Johnson carried out a good deal of work there between 1782 and 1794.[2] He was also concerned in the building of three Houses of Correction in Essex. That at Halstead had been begun by Hillyer, and Johnson completed it.[3] The Barking House of Correction was in progress, under Johnson's supervision, in 1791.[4] His last work was the House at Chelmsford, which stood in the middle of the High Street, opposite to Springfield Lane. It was begun in 1802 and finished in 1807.[5]

The building at Chelmsford was not without its critics. One member of the House of Correction Committee went so far as to take the opinions of another architect and of a mason upon it, and he brought their comments before the Committee. They alleged that the House of Correction was, as we should now say, "jerry-built", and that the walls were so thin that it would be an easy matter for a prisoner to loosen the bricks and so escape. Johnson made a detailed reply to these charges, which entirely satisfied the Committee and the Court of Quarter Sessions.[6]

This was not the only criticism that was passed upon his work. He does not seem to have been entirely successful as a builder of bridges. In 1787 he rebuilt Moulsham Bridge at Chelmsford, replacing the medieval structure, which had three arches, by the single-arched bridge that

[1] *The State of the Prisons* (ed. 3, 1784), 259-60.
[2] Essex Record Office, Q/FAC. 5/1 ; Q/SO. 14, page 135 ; Q/SO. 15, page 424 ; G. A. Cooke, *Topographical and Statistical Description of the County of Essex* (n.d.), 99.
[3] Essex Record Office, Q/FAC. 5/1 ; Q/SO. 13, page 264.
[4] Essex Record Office, Q/SO. 15, page 39.
[5] Essex Record Office, Q/SO. 18, page 374 ; Q/SO. 19, pages 71, 335, 603.
[6] Essex Record Office, Q/SO. 20, pages 18-24.

still spans the river. The new bridge was shorter than the old, the river being artificially narrowed through the tipping of bricks and other rubbish down its banks, under Johnson's instructions. It was alleged that this increased flooding in winter, and criticism was so strong that after Johnson's death the great engineer Telford was asked to examine the bridge and report upon it. He did so in 1824, but the text of his report seems to have disappeared. Whatever he may have said, the bridge still stands unaltered. From an aesthetic point of view we may be thankful, for it is a most graceful structure; and happily it is now scheduled as an ancient monument.

Another bridge undertaken by Johnson at the same time was the very important one at the foot of Gun Hill in the parish of Dedham, carrying the main road from London to Ipswich over the Stour, out of Essex into Suffolk. At this point the river runs very close to the steep southern side of its valley, and in a wet winter it is liable to overflow its banks. Johnson rebuilt the bridge about 1787;[2] but on 10 February 1795 it was blown up by the pressure of water in a great flood. In his official report on the disaster, dated 14 April 1795, Johnson put the blame on the county magistrates of Suffolk. He pointed out that in 1785, when the rebuilding of the bridge had been under discussion, the magistrates of Essex and Suffolk had met, and it had then been agreed that the whole cost of the bridge should be borne by Essex, but that Suffolk should pay for the building of an arch under the causeway that led up to the bridge from the north. By this means

---

[1] Criticism of the bridge will be found in a bundle of papers, mostly dating from 1818 to 1824, in the Essex Record Office: D/Do p. Telford's report was read at the Court of Quarter Sessions on 22 September 1824: Q/SO. 28, page 608.

[2] The rebuilding was in progress in 1787, and Johnson reported on 10 February 1795 that it had been finished seven or eight years: Essex Record Office, Q/SO. 14, page 135; Q/SO. 16, page 19.

it was thought that the pressure on the bridge would be relieved in time of flood. In spite of this undertaking, the arch was not built.

The Essex magistrates accepted Johnson's explanation, put the chief blame on their brethren of Suffolk, and proceeded to demand that they should now carry out their bargain as a necessary condition of the rebuilding of the bridge. The matter was urgent, because the Postmaster-General was threatening to indict the county of Essex at the assizes for its failure to maintain the bridge in repair. He was willing to suspend action, however, if the matter was settled quickly.[1]

That was all one to the magistrates of Suffolk. On 28 May they met and refused to do anything, and they maintained this attitude for three months more. They gave way, however, on 22 August, agreeing to build a bridge on the Suffolk side of the causeway and instructing their surveyor, Mr. John Doughty, to meet Johnson and examine the details on the spot. But it was not until 13 July 1796 that Johnson was able to report that " Dedham Bridge is completed in a neat and substantial manner ".[2] This bridge was replaced by an iron one about 1845, and by the existing concrete structure in 1928. The present Surveyor to the County of Essex tells me that he does not believe the arch under the causeway was ever, in fact, built ; and he considers that the breaking of Johnson's first bridge was probably due to a defect in its construction.[3]

One other work undertaken by Johnson in his official capacity as Surveyor to the County of Essex remains to be considered, and it is the most important of them all. At

[1] Essex Record Office, Q/SO. 16, pages 19-23.
[2] Essex Record Office, Q/SO. 16, pages 51, 104-5, 254.
[3] Plans of two other bridges, designed by Johnson, are preserved in the Essex Record Office : one at Widford of 1803 (Q/AB b 3), and one at Akingford of 1806 (Q/AB b 4). Johnson reported on 13 January 1807 that the Akingford bridge was finished (S/SO. 19, page 602).

the time of his appointment the business of the county was transacted in a little old Shire House, which was quite inadequate for the purpose, and in 1788 the county magistrates could endure it no longer. At the Michaelmas Court of Quarter Sessions they resolved " that the present Shire House is not in a fit condition for transacting the public business of the county ; that it is expedient and necessary to repair the Shire House or to build a new one and to provide a grand jury room, a room for witnesses, and a place for depositing the county records ". A committee of magistrates was set up to consider the means of carrying out this resolution, and the County Surveyor was ordered to examine the building and make a report to the Committee at its first meeting, to be held on 10 November 1788.[1] Johnson's first report was that the building could be " put into such condition as to last some years at an expense not exceeding £200 " ;[2] but the Committee told the magistrates at the Epiphany Sessions in 1789 that the old House could not be satisfactorily repaired and that Johnson had produced plans for a new one, estimated to cost not more than £8,918. It was then determined to accept his advice and to build a new Shire Hall to his design. On 10 July 1789 a contract was made for the work with Messrs. John Johnson, junior (the architect's son), Joseph Andrews, and William Horsfall.[3]

The Shire Hall was completed in 1791, to the great satisfaction of the Essex magistrates. When the Committee made their final report to the Court of Quarter Sessions at Epiphany 1792, they stated that the work had been " completed in the most perfect and elegant manner, with a saving of near £2,000 under the original estimate ", and it was decided to present Johnson with a piece of plate

[1] Essex Record Office, Q/SO. 14, page 230.
[2] Essex Record Office, Q/AS. 2/4.
[3] Essex Record Office, Q/SO. 14, pages 260, 24.

of the value of 100 guineas to mark the county's appreciation of his services.[1]

Johnson seems to have considered the Shire Hall at Chelmsford his most important work, for he published a thin folio volume of *Plans, Sections, and Perspective Elevation* of the building.[2] Its exterior has not been much altered. It is built of white brick, faced with Portland stone, its square severe lines relieved by panels of sculpture designed by John Bacon, R.A., and executed in Coade's artificial stone. Inside, the ground floor has been completely rearranged and refurnished, but the great room upstairs remains in its original state. Here the most beautiful feature is the rich and elaborate ceiling. The marble fireplaces at each end are ornamented with tablets by J. C. F. Rossi (1762-1839).[3]

One other undertaking of Johnson's in Chelmsford must be mentioned, though it was not a part of his official work. On 17 January 1800 the greater part of the nave and the south aisle of Chelmsford church collapsed. It was a sudden disaster, due to some workmen who were opening a vault and thereby undermined the inadequate foundations of the south arcade. A private Act of Parliament was secured to enable a special rate to be levied for the rebuilding of the church, and Johnson was invited to

---

[1] Nichols, i. 528 note, quoting *Chelmsford Chronicle*, 13 January 1792. There is some mystery about the cost of the building. Johnson's original estimate, as we have seen, was £8,918. But the total cost was given on 19 July 1793 as £13,789 14s. 9d. (Essex Record Office, Q/AS. 2/4). I do not know how this discrepancy is to be explained.

[2] The publisher was John Nichols, the Leicestershire historian. No date is printed on the title-page of the book. The *Dictionary of National Biography* (under Johnson) asserts that it appeared in 1808, but this short article is so inaccurate that its statements have to be taken with caution: it says, for instance, that Johnson was born in 1754 (instead of 1732), that he was Surveyor to the county of Essex for 26 years (instead of 30), and that he built the Consanguinitarium after he returned to Leicester, whereas its foundation in fact dates from 1795, twenty years before he retired from London.

[3] Rossi received £21 for the work: Essex Record Office, Q/AS. 2/4. He was the son of an Italian, who practised as a doctor at Mountsorrel and married a Leicester woman.

draw up the plans. Between 20 June 1802 and 14 February 1806 sums totalling £3,110 17s. od. were paid to him— not, of course, solely as professional fees : no doubt he acted also as paymaster for some or all of the workmen, in a way that then was very common.[1]  In rebuilding the church Johnson added galleries at the west end and over the aisles ; and he put a new roof on to the nave, which still remains, a unique and lovely monument of the early Gothic Revival. It is interesting to note that the design has been generally approved even by antiquaries who usually dislike the work of that period.[2]

Johnson did not retire from his office until he had reached the age of eighty, in 1812.  The county's formal farewell of him may be given in the words of the Order Book of Quarter Sessions :  " This Court having received and read a letter from John Johnson Esquire, Surveyor of the County Works, announcing his intention to resign that office at the next Michaelmas Quarter Sessions on account of his late illness and great age, do unanimously resolve that the thanks of this Court be given to the said John Johnson Esquire for his long, active, faithful, and meritorious services to this county during the space of more than thirty years, and doth order that such resolution be entered into the records of this county and that a copy thereof, signed by the Clerk of the Peace, be transmitted to Mr. Johnson and inserted three times in the *Chelmsford Chronicle* and the *Essex Herald* and also in the *County Chronicle* ".[3]

---

[1] Chelmsford churchwardens' accounts.
[2] See, for example, J. C. Cox, *Essex* (" Little Guide " : ed. 3, 1913), 113 ; and G. Worley, *Essex : a Dictionary of the County mainly Ecclesiological* (1915), 23. For pictures of the church as it appeared after the crash of 1800, see W. Chancellor, *A Short History of the Cathedral Church of St. Mary the Virgin, Chelmsford* (1938), 14, 16. Another, showing the interior in 1850, much as it had been when Johnson finished his work, appears on page 27.
[3] Essex Record Office, Q/SO. 21, page 588.

Johnson's work in Leicester demands equally close attention. His earliest undertaking seems to have been the Town Gaol. It replaced an earlier building, on which Howard had commented unfavourably.[1] Architecturally, it was suitably severe and economical. It stood in High Cross Street and was demolished after the completion of the new gaol in Welford Road in 1828.[2]

Johnson's next work was a very curious group of buildings. It comprised first a block of four handsome houses, which he put up " in Southgate Street, near the Water-house pump . . . on the spot where he was born " ; and behind, partly screened by this block, the Consanguini-tarium. This was a charitable foundation for the benefit of his relatives. It was a battlemented stone building, with Gothic windows, containing five small houses.[3]

The Consanguinitarium was endowed by means of an indenture of bargain and sale of 24 January 1795. Under this instrument Johnson granted to a group of his relatives, who were to act as trustees, the building itself and an estate at Lubbenham in Leicestershire yielding a rent of £70 a year, which was to maintain the institution. The relatives named were the architect's son John, described as " of Berners Street, architect " ; his brother-in-law, Joseph Springthorpe of Leicester, corn-chandler ;[4] the Rev. Charles Johnson of South Stoke, Somerset ; Joseph Johnson of Upper Belgrave Place, bachelor of physic ; William Johnson of Leicester, nurseryman ; and Joseph Springthorpe of Leicester, corn-chandler.

The trustees were to be responsible for running the Consanguinitarium and for nominating its five occupants,

---

[1] Nichols, i. 531 ; Howard, *State of the Prisons* (ed. 3, 1784), 313.
[2] There is a view of Johnson's gaol in Plate XXVIII of the first volume of Nichols' *History*, opposite page 326.
[3] Nichols, i. 528. Engravings showing both blocks of building appear in Plate XXXV of the first volume.
[4] Mr. J. F. J. Goodacre was kind enough to point out this relationship to me.

who were all to be related to Johnson. The institution
was governed by strict rules, laid down by the founder
himself. Each inmate was to receive 4s. 6d. a week, together
with a ton of coal a year. Rules III and IV must be quoted :
" III. No inhabitant to keep either dog, cat, fowls, or
rabbits, nor any other animal that may be a nuisance : nor
to carry on any business in his or her dwelling that
may render the same unseemly. IV. No inhabitant to be
allowed to keep any inmate, or any visitor to sleep with him
or her, on pain of dismission." None of them was to be
out, or to have visitors, later than 10 o'clock in summer, or
9 o'clock in winter, on pain of a sixpenny fine. The utmost
care was taken to ensure neighbourly co-operation. When
one of the inhabitants died, all the other inhabitants were
to pay for his or her burial : the females were to attend
on each other, and on the males, in case of sickness, " or
to be dismissed ". Even the washing days were prescribed
in the rules : House no. 1 was to do its washing on Monday,
House no. 2 on Tuesday, and so on up to the fifth house
on Friday. From such a founder, we need not be surprised
at Rule VIII—" No child or children to be admitted into
the lawn, on any account "—or at the final rule (XII),
with its precepts of majestic morality : " It is presumed
that every kind of good order and decorum among the
inhabitants of the Consanguinitarium will exist ; that they
will be neat and clean in their apartments and dress ; vie
with each other in acts of friendly assistance to their resident
relatives ; that they will also duly attend public worship,
at such place as is most congenial to their conscience, and
give praise to the Great Author of the Universe, for
enabling and permitting the Founder of these dwellings
to have the pleasure of giving the comforts they afford to
them. But should any be so lost to themselves as to sow
strife and discord, or by abusive words or actions render

the meek-minded unhappy, they will be removed for ever from their places of residence ".

By his will, dated 12 January 1811 and proved in 1815, Johnson devised the four houses that stood in front of the Consanguinitarium to his brother William, to a niece, a nephew, and a great-nephew, charging annual sums of £4 or £6 upon them, which were to go to the further endowment of the Consanguinitarium.[1]

We now come to Johnson's most important work in Leicester, the County Rooms. They have an interesting history. They were originally undertaken as an hotel, but the proprietor found his resources inadequate to its completion, and his holding was taken over by a group of private gentlemen in 1799 or 1800. In August 1800 it was stated that £3,300 was still required to finish the hotel and assembly rooms, with the outlying buildings, tap, stables, etc., and that if this sum was not raised within a month the property would have to be sold.[2] A subscription list was opened for furnishing the public rooms so that they could be opened in time for the races on 17 September. Presumably the money was found somehow, for the assembly room was used for the first time on that day.[3]

The best contemporary description of the building when it was new is that given in Nichols' *History of Leicestershire* :

" The front of the hotel, which name it bears, having been originally designed for that purpose, may, from the grandeur of its windows, its statues, basso relievo, and other decorations, be justly considered as the first modern architectural adornment of the town.

---

[1] *Report of the Commissioners to inquire into Charities : Leicester* (1838), 100-2. The Consanguinitarium has now been removed to Earl Howe Street. Johnson's buildings have wholly disappeared.
[2] *Leicester Journal*, 8 August 1800.
[3] ibid., 19 September 1800.

" A room, whose spacious dimensions (being 75 feet by 33, and 30 feet high) and elegant decorations adapt it in a distinguished manner for scenes of numerous and polished society, is appropriated to the use of the public balls. The entrance is in the centre of the side wall, over which is a spacious orchestra, projecting a small way into the room. It is of a semi-circular plan, domed, and carried back over the landing of the stairs : the access to it is by a back staircase. The ceiling of the room is arched and formed into compartments ; three of which are large circles, decorated with the allegorical paintings of Aurora, Urania, and Luna. At each end is a chimney, over which is a painting, in a compartment, of an aërial figure in a dazzling attitude : there are also two others, in compartments, on a side wall. On each side of the chimneys are niches, in which are beautiful figures, from the models of Bacon. Mr. Johnson employed Mr. Ramsey Reinagle[1] to execute the paintings, who has done great justice to his appointment ; but they have suffered much from the damp, for want of fire. Beside the eight beautiful lustres, branches of lights are held by four statues from the designs of Bacon. Mr. Rossi, R.A., was employed (partly on account of his mother being a native of Leicester, but much more so from his superior merit as an artist) to execute the two figures in the front of the building (Comic and Lyric Muses) and the bas reliefs between the windows.

" Uniting under the same roof every convenience for the gratification of taste and the amusement of the mind, a coffee-room handsomely furnished, and supplied with all the London papers, affords the gentlemen of the town and country, as well as the stranger, to whom its door is open, an agreeable and commodious resort."[2]

[1] R. R. Reinagle (1775-1862), President of the Old Water-Colour Society 1808-1812, R.A. 1823-1848.
[2] Nichols, i. 533-4.

It is interesting to note that Johnson, Bacon, and Rossi worked together here as at the Shire Hall in Chelmsford.

A view of the building appeared in 1800, engraved by J. Walker. It was from this engraving that the print in Nichols' *History* was taken. The façade has not been much altered since it was finished, except in one unfortunate respect : the original small panes have been taken out of the windows and large, ugly sheets of plate glass substituted.

It does not seem that the Rooms prospered under their original management, and in 1817 they were sold to the county. At the Lent assizes of that year the grand jury " represented to the Justices of the Peace of this county the inconvenience of the Judges' lodgings during their attendance at the assizes and . . . recommended the purchasing a house or building with suitable accommodation for the purpose ".[1] The Assembly Rooms were at hand, and the transaction went through very speedily. A private Act of Parliament had to be secured to enable the money to be raised from the county rates. It is interesting to note that the petition put up to Parliament for this purpose stated that the county was in need not only of Judges' Lodgings but of a " place of deposit and safe custody of public records ". It is to be supposed that the Rooms were used for this purpose until the Castle was bought by the county in 1888. I have not been able to discover what price the county paid, but at the Quarter Sessions of Easter 1818 it was agreed that a sum not exceeding £1,500 should be spent on repairs and alterations, and a similar sum on furniture for the use of the judges.

The work of adaptation began in the summer of 1817— well before the Act of Parliament had been secured. The builder who was in charge of the work, Joshua Harrison,

---

[1] County Record Office, Leicester : Quarter Sessions Minute Book, 1809-1818—under 15 July 1817.

at first maintained that the ceiling of the ballroom was unsafe and would have to be taken down, but he afterwards agreed that it could be repaired : it still survives. If Harrison's estimates are to be trusted, however, a startling amount of work had to be done to put the building in order, even though it had been completed less than twenty years. The window-frames were " so damaged by the admission of wet that they must be partially renewed ", " new ceilings are needed in almost all the rooms ", and so on. It looks as if the Rooms had been suffering severely from neglect.

By the spring of 1819 the work was complete down to its details, to the knives and forks and linen that had been bought for the judges' use. It may be added that the word " Hotel " was obliterated over the porch, and the stones on which " Assembly Rooms " were cut at the top were turned round : the words can still be seen from the inside of the parapet.[1]

Adjoining the County Rooms on the south side stood another building by Johnson : the Theatre, which was opened a few months earlier, on 17 March 1800,[2] and was replaced by the present Theatre Royal, on the same site, in 1836. It was very small, and though Nichols gallantly did his best for it by describing it as " neatly and commodiously fitted up, nearly on the plan of the London houses ", it was found inconvenient and nobody seems to have regretted its disappearance.[3]

One other project of Johnson's connected with Leicester must be mentioned, even though it was not carried out. In 1792 he produced a plan of a Brunswick Square, which,

---

[1] These details of the purchase and conversion of the Rooms are taken from miscellaneous papers at the County Record Office, Leicester.

[2] *Leicester Journal*, 14 and 21 March 1800. A prologue was written for the opening night by Miss Susanna Watts (the author of *A Walk through Leicester*, 1804) : it is printed in full in the *Journal* for 28 March 1800.

[3] See the tart comment on it in Curtis, *Topographical History*, 113.

says Nichols, " was intended to have been formed on the
site of the Horse Fair (Johnson's Garden), an extensive
plot of ground, at that time the property of the corporation
of Leicester. In the area of the Square was to have been
St. Margaret's chapel ; on two of the sides beautiful streets,
to be named George Street and Charlotte Street, after
their present Majesties. A Royal Terrace would have filled
the side looking towards the London Road ; and a new
Town Hall, opening into Millstone Lane, was to have
filled the fourth side. Had this plan taken effect, it would
have been creditable to the town ; in which no place can
be put in competition, either for public convenience, or a
display of corporate magnificence and civic grandeur."[1]
What an opportunity was missed here ! It was a chance
of giving the town a really fine and well-planned centre,
and once gone it never returned.

In addition to his public work in Essex and Leicester,
Johnson also designed a number of other buildings in the
South of England and Wales. A list of them is given in
Nichols' *History of Leicestershire* : it will be found in
Appendix I, pages 242-245. With the exception of
Wimbledon church, which he rebuilt in 1787, his work is
wholly domestic. As we should expect, most of it is to
be found in London and Essex ; but he built Killerton for
the Aclands in Devonshire and two houses in Glamorgan.
None of his houses is on a great scale. Those that are
most characteristic of him—Kingsthorpe in Northamptonshire or Langford Grove by Maldon—are of a moderate
size, severe and plain. Occasionally he went in for more
elaborate decoration, as at his noble Woolverstone Hall,
near Ipswich. But on the whole I think it would be fair
to say that he was at his best as a civic architect. His public

---

[1] Nichols, i. 531.

buildings at Chelmsford and Leicester are the most successful of his works.

Johnson retired, as we have seen, from his position as County Surveyor of Essex at Michaelmas 1812. His friends showed that they were prepared to give him something more than fair words. The official resolution of the Court of Quarter Sessions in Essex refers to his " late illness," but it appears that that was not his only trouble : he had financial worries to face as well. The story is not wholly clear, for the evidence is disjointed and fragmentary.[1] In January 1813 a body of 59 subscribers undertook to pay him an annual sum for the rest of his life. This seems to have amounted to £105, but in the course of 1813 Johnson's representatives in Leicester wrote on his behalf to acknowledge two further sums totalling £371. Through them Johnson expressed his gratitude and pleasure to the subscribers. Their gift, he says, " is such a test of their esteem and good opinion of his conduct during his holding the office of Surveyor to the county that will ever remain on his mind while memory lasts." One further point emerges from this correspondence. His son John died, in 1812 or early in 1813, and left his father an annuity of £200. But his " affairs are in such a deranged state that it is likely to be twelve years before they can be adjusted."

Johnson's prosperous career, then, came to a pathetic conclusion, in long illness and adversity. He died where he had been born, in Southgate Street at Leicester, on 17 August 1814. He was buried in St. Martin's. In the south quire aisle there is a monument to Johnson's parents, designed by himself and executed by Bacon : his own death is baldly commemorated in an inscription on its base.

[1] It is to be found in a bundle of papers in the Essex Record Office : D/Dke. F10.

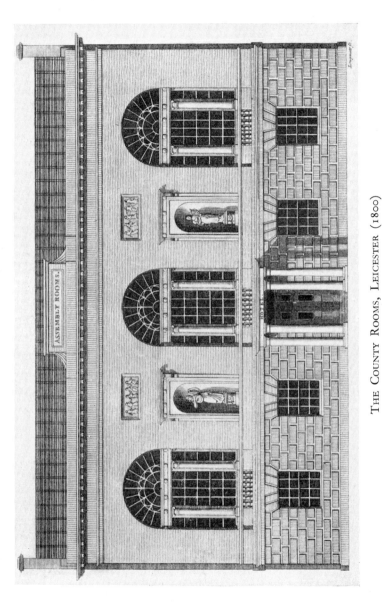

THE COUNTY ROOMS, LEICESTER (1800)

From an engraving by Longmate in Nichols' *History and Antiquities of the Town and County of Leicester* (1795-1815)

WILLIAM JESSOP
From a drawing by George Dance the younger (1796)
in the National Portrait Gallery

Two obituary notices of Johnson appeared in the press, discreet and impersonal.[1]

One other point in his career remains to be recorded. In his *Topographical History of the County of Leicester*, which was published in 1831, the Rev. J. Curtis refers to Johnson as "architect and banker ".[2] I have not succeeded in tracing Johnson's financial activities : the word " banker ", indeed, has a very vague significance at this date. But it brings us back to the most interesting problem of his life. How did he make his way in youth and early middle age ? Above all, how did he acquire the competent fortune that enabled him to build and endow the Consanguinitarium in 1795 ?

There apparently exists only one portrait of Johnson : a very small medallion, now in the County Rooms at Leicester. His personality remains almost completely hidden from us. Almost, but not quite : it is surely possible to detect some hint of the man himself from the strange tenacity of his feeling for his relations (which led him in the end to retire to Southgate Street to die among them) and from the fussy, meticulous rules he laid down for his Consanguinitarium. But if he himself remains a shadow, his career is of considerable interest : for it shows us something of the work of a forgotten class of public servants—the County Surveyors of the eighteenth century.

[1] *Leicester Journal*, 16 September 1814; *Gentleman's Magazine*, vol. 84, part ii, page 296.
[2] Curtis, 113.

# WILLIAM JESSOP, CIVIL ENGINEER

WE KNOW curiously little about the lives of our great engineers. They contributed at least as much as any other single group of men to the industrial triumphs of Britain in the eighteenth and nineteenth centuries : yet not much has been done to commemorate them worthily. The classic account of them, as a group, is the *Lives of the Engineers* by Samuel Smiles, which, for all its *naïve* moralising, remains as readable and in its main lines as acceptable as when it first appeared in 1857-1868. Smiles attacked his great subject with immense industry and with some technical knowledge : he was Secretary to the South Eastern Railway and so knew about a part at least of his subject from the inside. And he had the advantage of writing while the story was still recent. Robert Stephenson was still alive when his first volume was published : he was able to draw on personal recollection to supplement the facts recorded on paper.

But Smiles's book stands alone. There have been good biographies of single engineers since—Sir Alexander Gibb's *Story of Telford*, for example ; and competent technical studies, like Mr. Robert Young's *Timothy Hackworth* and Messrs. Dickinson and Titley's *Trevithick*. But the number even of these separate studies is not great, and none of them achieves Smiles's blend of readability and knowledge.[1]

[1] Cf. Chapter xxii, " Desiderata of Industrial Biography," in C. R. Fay, *English Economic History mainly since* 1700 (1940).

The reasons are soon discerned. In the first place, the task is far from an easy one. Smiles's achievement is more remarkable perhaps than we realise. To make the story of an engineer's life interesting and comprehensible as history, while at the same time treating intelligently the technical problems that confronted him : that would be a difficult literary feat to perform even if the materials were copious and satisfactory. But they are neither. The record of an engineer's life is to be found primarily in the works he carried through, just as an architect's must be discussed primarily in terms of his buildings. Any one who has ever studied the life of an architect will know what difficulties there are in the way of compiling even a bare list of his works. Yet there is much more collateral evidence to go upon there than with an engineer : a fuller correspondence with his employers, his plans and elevations, which are often preserved, the evidence (open to endless dispute, but not on that account to be ignored) of style. The early engineers, on the other hand, seldom committed much to paper : one thinks of the great Brindley, who was largely or wholly illiterate, of Blind Jack Metcalf of Knaresborough, of the letters of George Stephenson, terse, uncommunicative, rare. For the foundation of our knowledge of their work we usually have to depend first of all upon contemporary statements, made by those who had good means of finding out the truth. We can then begin to check and amplify the story from other sources : from the records of the companies that employed the engineers, from their works themselves.

The process can be well illustrated from the life of William Jessop (1745-1814). He is a considerable figure of the Industrial Revolution—or he would be if he had had justice done to him. But as it is, only one account of him has hitherto been written, a brief memoir by a fellow-

engineer, Samuel Hughes, which appeared in 1844.[1]  He
is not included in the *Dictionary of National Biography* : that
great work is particularly defective in the field of industrial
history.  In this essay I wish to collect the main facts that are
known of his professional career, to indicate the remarkable
range of his work.  I hope this may lay some of the foundations on which a more complete memoir may be constructed.

Like his distinguished predecessor Newcomen, Jessop
was a Devon man by birth, though not by descent.  It is
probable that his family came from Derbyshire, where
the name is frequently met with—the county in which he
himself eventually made his home.[2]  His father, Josias
Jessop, was foreman of shipwrights at Plymouth Dockyard
and acted virtually as Smeaton's resident engineer during
the building of the third Eddystone lighthouse.[3]  William
was born and brought up in Plymouth, until his father
died in 1761.  Smeaton then took him under his guardian-
ship, and he gave the young man his start in life as an
engineer : in 1774 we find him submitting an official
opinion on " Mr. Jessop's Report on the Tyrone Canal ".[4]
That is the only detail I have so far recovered of Jessop's
early life, but he is also said to have been employed in
improving the navigation of various rivers in Yorkshire
and of the Trent.[5]  He next appears in 1789 reporting on
two schemes for navigation from Lechlade to Oxford and
from Oxford to Dorchester.[6]

He was already associated at this time as a canal and

[1] It is printed in John Weale's *Quarterly Papers on Engineering*, vol. i, and cited
here as " Hughes ".

[2] For Jessops in Derbyshire, see, for instance, the *Journal of the Derbyshire
Archaeological and Natural History Society*, ii. 152, iv. 147, xvii. 33.

[3] John Smeaton, *A Narrative of the Building of the Eddystone Lighthouse* (ed. 2,
1813), 30, 45 ; Smiles, *Lives of the Engineers* (1861-1862), ii. 30-1, 34.

[4] ibid., ii. 197 n. ; *Reports by the late John Smeaton* (1812), ii. 278-9.

[5] Hughes, 2.

[6] His reports are printed in *Reports of the Engineers appointed by the Commissioners
of the Navigation of the River Thames and Isis to survey the state of the said Navigation
from Lechlade to Day's Lock* (1791).  A copy of this is in the Bodleian Library :
Vet. A. 5. d. 164.

dock engineer with Benjamin Outram; and in 1790 he and Outram, together with two other partners, formed the Butterley Company, near Ripley in Derbyshire.[1] This developed into one of the great industrial combines of the nineteenth century, equally important for its ironworks and its collieries. In this area Jessop built a good many canals during the last decade of the eighteenth century.[2] One of them, the Cromford Canal, contributed greatly to the development of the Butterley Company.

In 1791 Jessop was employed on the plans for the Foss Navigation in the North Riding of Yorkshire.[3] Next year he was called upon to advise on the construction of the Grand Junction Canal, the great waterway that runs from the Oxford Canal at Braunston in Northamptonshire to the Thames at Brentford. He was mainly responsible for its actual building, and it is usually reckoned as his most important work.[4] Towards the end of 1793 he was appointed consulting engineer to the Ellesmere Canal Company.[5] The plan of the canal has been produced by Thomas Telford, a young Scot twelve years his junior. This was their first association, and they worked together for the rest of Jessop's life. Telford was unquestionably the man of greater genius; but he came to place the firmest reliance on Jessop's judgment, and he consulted him very frequently. Telford's biographer remarks that " Jessop's report and his advice were valuable because they were always constructive; and he never suggested an alternative

---

[1] For the early development of this great company see S. Glover, *History of the County of Derby* (1829), i. 231-2. See also R. H. Mottram and C. Coote, *Through Five Generations : the History of the Butterley Company* (1950).
[2] The Leicester Navigation, the Erewash, Cromford, and Nottingham Canals : J. Farey, *General View of the Agriculture of Derbyshire* (1811-1817), iii. 365, 399; J. Priestley, *Historical Account of the Navigable Rivers, Canals, and Railways of Great Britain* (1831), 173, 403.
[3] Priestley, 274.
[4] Hughes, 16 ; Priestley, 312.
[5] ibid., 238 ; Sir A. Gibb, *The Story of Telford* (1935), 29.

from any conscious or unconscious desire to exhibit his own learning."[1]

From this time onwards we have at least the names of the chief projects on which Jessop was engaged. In the years 1793-1799 he was building the Barnsley Canal, in collaboration with Elias Wright and Mr. Gott.[2] In 1794 he estimated for the Ashby-de-la-Zouch Canal, together with Robert Whitworth, who actually carried out the work.[3] A year later he presented a report on a canal (which came to nothing) from Newcastle to Maryport in Cumberland and in the following summer another on the drainage of the River Hull.[4] He is also said to have been associated with the building of the Grand Western Canal, from Taunton to Topsham, which was authorised in 1796.[5] designing the great West India Docks in London, and then in 1802 suggesting improvements in the harbour of Bristol.[6] In 1804 he was called in by Telford to give advice on the Caledonian Canal: he visited it that autumn, and annually for the next eight years. Half the ironwork for the lock gates was supplied by the Butterley Company. From 1810 onwards he was associated once again with Telford in the improvement of Aberdeen harbour.[7]

These are the greatest works with which his name is connected. It is as a canal engineer that he should be chiefly remembered. He made at least one valuable contribution to the technique of canal-building: he was the first man to suggest the use of reservoirs for supplying canals where no natural streams of adequate size were

---

[1] Gibb, 94.
[2] Priestley, 55.
[3] ibid., 31.
[4] A copy of the former is in the Bodleian (Gough Adds. Northumberland 8vo 60), and of the latter in the London Library (P 2184).
[5] C. Hadfield, *British Canals* (1950), 119-21.
[6] Gibb, 338 ; Hughes, 25, 30-1.
[7] Gibb, 94, 149 ; *Life of Thomas Telford* (1838), 63.

available.[1]  But he was also concerned in the development
of railways, and here too he initiated an important advance.
Most of the early English railways were short lines, intended
simply as feeders for waterways.  For one of these, the
Loughborough and Nanpantan Railway in Leicestershire,
Jessop designed and cast the first rails made wholly of
iron (1789): the complete elimination of wood was an
essential step in the development of the rail, strengthening
it to bear heavier loads.[2]

He has been credited, however, with another invention,
to which he has no claim.  The writers of the official
history of the Butterley Company have recently told us
that " Jessop took the railway a whole age farther.  He saw
the awkwardness of a flanged rail when a junction had to
be made, and therefore he transferred the flange from the
rail to the wheels of the wagon ".[3]  Some years ago Mr.
Charles E. Lee showed conclusively that this story is
based on a misunderstanding.  The earliest English railways
were all of the kind we know today, designed for vehicles
with flanged wheels.  It was only in the last quarter of the
eighteenth century that the L-shaped plateway appeared,
in the neighbourhood of Sheffield, and then for a clear
and special purpose : to accommodate wagons with flat
tyres, which could run either on the plateway or on the
ordinary road.  " We thus see the plateway ", writes Mr.
Lee, " not as a stage in the evolution of the modern railway,
certainly not as the earliest form of track, and not even as
as a retrograde step in permanent-way construction."[4]

Jessop was not in truth an innovator here—or he was
one only in a limited sense.  The plateway may have
become established as the standard one in the North

[1] Hughes, 32.  He used reservoirs in his early work on the Cromford Canal :
Priestley, 173.
[2] Smiles, op. cit., iii. 8 ;  C. E. Lee, *The Evolution of Railways* (ed. 2, 1943), 76.
[3] Mottram and Coote, op. cit., 41.
[4] Lee, op. cit., 62.

Midlands during the preceding fifteen years (though even this guarded statement is open to dispute) ; and we know that it was warmly advocated by Jessop's colleague and partner, Benjamin Outram. Jessop's use of the edge-rail in the Loughborough and Nanpantan line may therefore have appeared a bold departure, when we can see now that he was only returning to an earlier practice and developing it.

In June 1801 Jessop was appointed engineer to a much more important concern, the Surrey Iron Railway—the first public railway, independent of any canal, to be built under an Act of Parliament.[1] He was responsible for the construction of the line, which ran from Wandsworth to Croydon. He was retained as engineer for the proposed southward continuation to Reigate and Godstone ;[2] and in 1803 he actually surveyed the ground for an extension to Portsmouth, but nothing came of this ambitious project.[3] He also designed at least one other railway—the line from Kilmarnock to Troon, built by the Duke of Portland, which was opened in 1810, and in the same year he was asked for his opinion on the projected Glasgow and Berwick Railway.[4]

Jessop was by now an old man, universally respected as one of the leading engineers of his time. It has been said that he had become, " no less than Smeaton had done before him, the great standing counsel of his profession ".[5] He suffered much from paralysis in his last years and died at Butterley on 18 November 1814, aged sixty-nine.[6] He

[1] Priestley, op. cit., 609.

[2] ibid., 182.

[3] C. E. Lee, " Early Railways in Surrey " : *Transactions of the Newcomen Society*, xxi. 50-60.

[4] C. F. Dendy Marshall, *A History of British Railways down to the year* 1830 (1938), 112, 133 ; Gibb, 144-5.

[5] Hughes, 31.

[6] ibid., 32 ; *The Times*, 22 November 1814.

had at least two sons, Josias and William, both of whom were also engineers.[1]

Three portraits of Jessop are extant. The first and the most convincing is the fine drawing by George Dance, dated 1796, in the National Portrait Gallery.[2] This is a delightful companion to Dance's later drawing of Jessop's fellow-engineer, John Rennie. The Institution of Civil Engineers possesses an oil portrait, showing him in old age.[3] There is also an engraving, which may perhaps have been made from this oil portrait, but bears no strong resemblance to it.[4]

There, then, is the skeleton of Jessop's career. But it is a skeleton, and little more. Though we can discover the works he was associated with, there are further, more recondite questions that remain unanswered. What sort of man was he personally? Level-headed, reliable, hard-working, physically strong—he must have been all these things to achieve what he did. But what besides? The authors of the history of the Butterley Company fall back upon conjecture. "We can fancy him," they say, "a sturdy figure in a stock and a stove-hat, driving a fast gig along execrable roads, cursing the mud, the darkness, and the toll-gate keeper, and perhaps spurred on to accelerate the realisation of his conception of swifter and more comfortable travel by his own discomfort and delays."[5] Perhaps: but that picture is wholly imaginary, and it hardly makes us see Jessop himself any more clearly.

There is, in truth, no need to enliven his biography by such fictional methods. His importance should by now be

---

[1] Priestley, 76, 457; Glover, vol. i, Appendix, p. 106; Farey, iii. 393.

[2] The engraving reproduced in Hughes's memoir seems to have been made from this drawing.

[3] Reproduced in Gibb, opposite p. 32.

[4] Reproduced in the *Transactions of the Newcomen Society*, vol. xxi, Plate xi. Jessop also figures in the group of "Eminent Men of Science, Living in the Years 1807-8", now in the National Portrait Gallery (No. 1075).

[5] Mottram and Coote, 42-3.

plain. He deserves to be remembered for the great works he carried through and for the Company he helped to found. But his career presents us with an interesting problem. How did he make his money? His start in life seems to have been extremely modest. Yet at forty-five he was able to join in establishing the Butterley Ironworks; we are told that he possessed coal interests at Kirkby-in-Ashfield;[1] he died in all the circumstances of prosperity, if not of wealth. If only we could discover more—some account books, a note of his investments, some receipts for the fees he was paid. Something of the kind may yet turn up. It would enable us to make a useful study of an important process in the history of the Industrial Revolution—that by which a technician, the servant of capitalists, managed to become a capitalist himself: a process repeated on a much grander scale by the Stephensons, father and son.[2]

[1] ibid., 48.
[2] Since this essay was in proof Mr. A. Temple Patterson has shown that Jessop was also responsible for the Leicester Navigation: see his paper, "The Making of the Leicestershire Canals," 1766 1814, in the *Transactions of the Leicestershire Archæological Society*, Vol. xxvii (1951).

# THE BUILDING OF THE WOODHEAD TUNNEL

THERE ARE in Great Britain four railway tunnels whose length exceeds three miles. They are the Severn Tunnel (4 miles 626 yards) and three that are cut through the Pennines : at Totley (3 miles 946 yards), Standedge (3 miles 57 yards), and Woodhead (3 miles 13 yards). The Woodhead Tunnel was the earliest of the four to be completed ; and though its construction was a less spectacular engineering feat than that of the Severn Tunnel, it happens that full and interesting details have been preserved of the conditions under which it was built. From them it is possible to compose a picture of the lives led by some of the railway labourers a century ago.[1]

The Sheffield, Ashton-under-Lyne, and Manchester Railway Company was formed in 1835. Its " preliminary notice " in the *Sheffield Iris* of 10 May referred to the great advantages that must accrue to a railway linking the West Riding with East Lancashire, and spoke of cutting through the Pennines by means of a tunnel two miles long. The Company obtained its Act of Parliament in 1837. Its first

[1] Some time after this essay was written Mr. R. A. Lewis published a paper on " Edwin Chadwick and the Railway Labourers " in the *Economic History Review*, vol. iii, No. 1 (1950), in which he covered much of the same ground as I cover here, though his treatment is rather fuller than mine. After some hesitation, I have decided to print my essay none the less, since my approach is somewhat different from Mr. Lewis's. I am primarily concerned with the building of the tunnel, he with the men who worked on it. But I should like to recommend readers of this essay to turn to Mr. Lewis's, for the two are complementary.

chairman was Lord Wharncliffe, who had been the champion of the Great Western Railway's Bill in the House of Lords in 1834-1835. He turned the first spadeful of earth on the railway at a slate quarry half-way between Saltersbrook and Woodhead on 1 October 1838. Construction went forward very slowly. Like most of the railway companies that were products of the " Little Mania " of 1836-1837, the Sheffield, Ashton, and Manchester found great difficulty in obtaining the necessary money in the succeeding years. Harvests were bad and money was hard to raise in the late thirties. However, work on the tunnel was begun in the autumn of 1838; the first contract was let to Messrs. Warwick, Smith, and Enderby; and soon some 400 men were employed on it. The Company's first engineer was C. B. Vignoles, who laid out the line and estimated the cost of the tunnel first at a little over £60,000 and then at nearly £100,000. He resigned in November 1839 in distressing circumstances and was succeeded by Joseph Locke. Locke was a personal opponent as well as a professional rival of Vignoles, and he at once set himself to reverse his predecessor's decisions. He immediately doubled the second estimate for the tunnel, contending that it was essential to line it with masonry throughout, which Vignoles had thought unnecessary. The previous system of dividing the work among many small contractors was abandoned, and the whole placed in the hands of large firms. Some improvement followed in the victualling arrangements for the men, though, as we shall see, they remained bad.

The first section of the line to be opened was that from Ardwick to Godley, in November 1841; it was extended to Old Dinting in the following December; in August 1844 it reached Woodhead; eleven months later the western section, from Dunford Bridge to Sheffield, was opened. The tunnel alone remained unfinished. Long before this there had been rumours that it never would be finished—even George Stephenson was said to have remarked that he would "*eat* the first loco-motive that passed through the projected tunnel of the Sheffield and Manchester Railway". Labour was hard to recruit, for it had got a bad name, largely owing to the slowness with which it went forward, and the Company was never out of financial difficulties. At length, however, in December

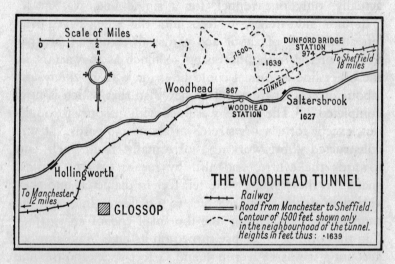

1845 the work was done. On Saturday the 20th it was inspected by General Pasley for the Board of Trade, who went through it " preceded in the train by a waggon, bearing six men with torches which were held to the roof and sides, the train proceeding very slowly, so that the nature of the work might be closely and carefully examined ". " We understood ", the *Manchester Guardian* added, " that General Pasley declared that it was one of the finest pieces of engineering he had ever seen." On the 22nd the directors and their friends passed through it; on the 23rd it was opened to the public, and trains began to run between Sheffield and Manchester.

In the absence of a technical press—the *Engineer* and the *Railway Engineer* were not yet born—the only contemporary descriptions of the engineering works are those given in the newspapers. The best account is perhaps that in the *Manchester Guardian* of 27 December. Here it is stated that the original intention had been to build two tunnels parallel, one on each side of the vertical shafts; actually, only one tunnel, for a single line, was made, " though side-arches, 6 feet into the side, have been left at intervals of about 200 yards, all through; so that in case of the traffic increasing so much as to warrant it, the other line of tunnel could be made with infinitely less labour or cost of time and money than that which is now completed ".[1] The tunnel was lined with masonry throughout, except for a short stretch of about 230 yards. It was constructed " by working horizontally from each end towards the centre, and also by means of five vertical shafts " : these shafts were ten feet in diameter, and they varied in depth from 408 feet to 546 feet. In shape the tunnel was " something like the small end of an egg "— " in the form of an ellipse turned on its end," said another account; it was 18 feet high and 15 feet wide, and the line through it rose uniformly in the Sheffield direction at 1 in 200. " At each end," said the *Sheffield Iris*, " is a castellated entrance, which gives a graceful finish to the unrivalled work." It was stated that 130 tons of gunpowder were used in its construction, and that the total cost was nearly £200,000.

The completion of the railway between Manchester

---

[1] As early as 1837 Lord Wharncliffe referred to the possibility of building a second tunnel, and stated that enough land had been acquired to enable this to be done without further purchase (*The Times*, 28 October 1837). It was made, and opened early in 1852.

and Sheffield was naturally regarded as a great event in Lancashire and Yorkshire. But outside the district through which the line passed it attracted small notice. This is a little surprising, for the Early Victorians took a keen interest in railway engineering, and the Woodhead tunnel was far longer than any other then existing in the country —its nearest competitor was the Box tunnel, 1 mile 1,452 yards long. Perhaps it was crowded out of the news; for that was an interesting December, what with the agitation for the repeal of the Corn Laws, the dispute with the United States over the Oregon boundary, the accident on the Norfolk Railway at Thetford, and the exciting suicide of Colonel Gurwood, the editor of Wellington's *Despatches*. For whatever reason, the opening of the tunnel passed almost unnoticed in London. The *Illustrated London News* recorded it briefly on 27 December 1845; the *Gentleman's Magazine* referred to it in its issue for the following March, and got the date of its opening wrong; *The Times* never even mentioned it. There the whole story might have ended, if it had not been for the activity and influence of one single-minded man.

Edwin Chadwick was a native of the district, born at Longsight in 1800. He was at this time secretary to the new poor-law commissioners, and well known as a fearless and determined enemy of inefficiency and social cruelty, wherever he saw it. A paper read to the Manchester Statistical Society by its president, a surgeon named John Roberton, called his attention to the shocking conditions under which the labourers who built the Woodhead tunnel had been employed; and immediately he decided to make the facts known to the world. Accordingly, he produced a substantial pamphlet of 55 pages, containing a detailed statement by Roberton on the subject, together with his own reflections on this and several similar cases which had

come to his notice.[1]  On 30 April 1846 Peel's government
was asked to appoint a Select Committee to inquire into
the conditions in which the railway labourers worked.  Sir
James Graham, the President of the Board of Trade, at
once agreed to the request.  Though the instances quoted
by the Hon. E. P. Bouverie, who moved for the Committee,
were drawn from Ireland, Chadwick's pamphlet had
certainly helped to bring the subject into notice : it was
constantly referred to in the evidence before the Committee.
The personnel of the Committee was strong (among its
members was George Hudson).   The witnesses who
appeared before it included Chadwick, Brunel, Peto,
Moorsom, and three who were more particularly concerned with the Sheffield, Ashton, and Manchester Railway :
W. A. Purdon, the resident engineer mainly responsible
for the tunnel ; H. L. Pomfret, a surgeon who had been
retained by the workmen's sick club while it was building ;
and Thomas Eaton, a navvy who had been employed on
it.  By the light of the evidence they gave and the facts
stated by Roberton we can gain some impression of the
conditions in which the men lived.  It must be remembered,
in their employers' defence, that they were working in a
remote and desolate spot, far from towns and even villages :
Woodhead itself consists of a few scattered farmhouses
and a small church ; Glossop is the nearest town, eight
miles to the south-west.  And the wages offered were
unusually high—miners got from 4s. to 5s. a day, joiners
5s., masons 6s.  The men were paid every nine weeks—
" to prevent their indulgence in hebdomadal excesses ",
says Locke's biographer.

The work was begun by sinking the tunnel shafts, in
the autumn of 1838.  It was only after Vignoles had made

---

[1] The pamphlet is undated.  It refers to the tunnel as completed, so that it
must have been finished after December 1845; but as it does not mention the
Select Committee, it cannot be put later than the following April.

representations to the directors of the company that tents were provided for the men: previously they had slept in the open. A little later on, some cottages were built for them, but this was found to be too expensive : the scheme was soon abandoned, and they were lodged in temporary huts instead. " The huts ", said Roberton, " are a curiosity. They are mostly of stones without mortar, the roof of thatch or of flags, erected by the men for their own temporary use, one workman building a hut in which he lives with his family, and lodges also a number of his fellow-workmen. In some instances as many as fourteen or fifteen men, we were told, lodged in the same hut ; and this at best containing two apartments, an outer and an inner, the former alone having a fire-place. Many of the huts were filthy dens, while some were whitewashed and more cleanly ; the difference, no doubt, depending on the turn and character of the inmates . . . At No. 1 shaft a workman told me that he has cut a road through the snow, from the door of his hut, four yards deep." Not all the men were accommodated in huts. Pomfret states that some of them slept in boiler-houses and stables, even when they were injured. Such living conditions provided the worst possible background for the work that the men were called on to perform. An agent of the Manchester Town Mission, who worked among the men for three months, " noticed that a number . . . had coughs, which they attributed to the moisture of the tunnel, wherewith every thread of their clothing was soaked before they had been a quarter of an hour at work. I said to a woman in a hut, ' How can ten or fourteen lodgers in one hut dry all their wet clothing by a single fire ? ' She answered that ' the clothes were seldom half dry '."

Not only were the men abominably housed : they were vilely fed. As they were far from towns, the provision

of food was a matter of some difficulty.  The authorities
fell back on the time-dishonoured system of " tommy-
shops " : that is to say, the right of selling provisions to
the men was let out to a contractor, who naturally made
his contract as profitable as possible.  The dearness and
badness of the goods struck every one, from the navvy
Thomas Eaton to the Manchester missionary, who noted
down the details and has preserved them for us.  The butter
purveyed was " of very indifferent odour " ;  brown sugar
" the worst sample " ;  treacle " the commonest ".   " But
the most surprising thing was the price of potatoes, namely
1s. 2d. the score.  Thinking that as the highest price in
Manchester was only eightpence, they were imposing on
my credulity, I inquired at several huts, widely apart, and
received the same answer,—1s. 2d. per score." This competent witness estimated that all prices were from 20 to
50 per cent. above those paid by people of a similar class
in Manchester.  It may be added that this state of affairs
cannot be excused by difficulties of transport, for this
information was collected in October 1845, when the
railway was open from Manchester and Sheffield to each
end of the tunnel.

But that is not all.  The work was necessarily of a
dangerous character : the authorities' callous disregard for
human suffering made it a great deal more dangerous than
it need have been.  It is not possible to state definitely how
many lives were lost during the construction of the tunnel :
the estimates range from 26 to 32.  The average number of
men employed was 400 during the first three years, after
which it rose to 1,000.  Chadwick had no difficulty in showing that this considerable mortality was completely unnecessary : he drew parallels with the mines in Cornwall, where,
he said, the work was more dangerous, yet it was most

unusual for a single life to be lost. Still more dreadful than the number of deaths were the statistics of injuries. Pomfret noted 23 compound fractures, 74 simple fractures, and 140 other " severe cases ". The totals must have been higher than this, since for a period of two years Pomfret dealt with casualties only on the western half of the tunnel, leaving those at the other end to a colleague, who supplied no details. Even as they stand, the figures are sufficiently shocking. A fair proportion of the serious injuries must have been permanently crippling ; among the " severe cases " are those of men who lost both eyes, and half a foot.

At no time during the construction of the tunnel was there a doctor living on the spot. The injured were attended by Pomfret, who lived at Hollingworth, some eight miles away. He himself stated that " two hours almost always elapsed before I saw my patient after the accident ". In those days there was neither dole nor compensation for the incapacitated. During their period of illness the men received an allowance of 8s. a week from a club to which they all subscribed 1½d. Suggestions that compensation might be paid by the employers to men disabled while working for them were rejected. Purdon thought such proposals " too hard ". For this argument Chadwick showed a characteristic contempt : " those who erect machines ", he said, " or conduct large and dangerous works, or undertake public conveyance, should be pecuniarily responsible for all their unavoidable, as well as for their avoidable consequences ". If employers were made liable in this way, he considered the effect " would in a very short time be to show that the large proportion of the so-called ' accidents ' are preventible ". Pomfret thought the remedy was less drastic : if the regulations concerning safety were enforced, instead of merely being made and forgotten, the number of accidents would inevitably fall. But his own experience in attempting to do something to check the mortality was scarcely encouraging. He made one suggestion to the contractor, that copper " stemmers " (rammers for putting dry clay on the top of gunpowder) would be less dangerous than iron ones. But " I was told that I was neither a contractor nor an engineer, and that it was not my province ".

How did the men react to this miserable and precarious life ? Most of them—it is not surprising—drank heavily ; they fought ; their morals were deplorable ; they stayed away from their work when they could afford to. Yet it is clear that both Pomfret and the missionary had a certain liking for them, and that they differed very little from their fellow-workers in the slums of the great cities ; that they were, in short, ordinary human beings in an extraordinarily grim situation.

After examining 31 witnesses over a period of two months, the Committee presented its Report (dated 28 July) to Parliament. For some reason it was not acted upon ; there was no debate on it ; it caused no public outcry ; neither company nor contractors attempted any defence, for no attack was made upon them. The Committee had done valuable work in ventilating the subject, but there it stopped. The condition of railway labourers was improving, under the influence of such contractors as Samuel Morton Peto, and there was never again such a terrible story as that of the Woodhead Tunnel. It is useless to attempt to blame any one for it. The company, as was usual at the time, let out the work to contractors, who found the men : the contractors were not legally obliged to do anything for their employees but to pay them their wages, and contractors were not philanthropists. The

Woodhead Tunnel stands as a monument to what has been well characterised as " the Bleak Age ".[1]

[1] This essay is based on contemporary evidence, contained in the following works : *Papers read before the Statistical Society of Manchester on the demoralisation and injuries occasioned by the want of proper regulations of labourers engaged in the construction and working of railways* (Manchester, n.d.) ; *Report of the Select Committee of the House of Commons on Railway Labourers* (Parliamentary Papers, 1846, vol. xiii, pp. 425-704), especially the evidence given by Pomfret (questions 1,046-1,226), Purdon (questions 1,544-1,632), and Eaton (questions 2,978-3,041) ; Joseph Devey, *The Life of Joseph Locke* (1862), 119-23 (this is an unreliable work, peppered with inaccuracies) ; O. J. Vignoles, *The Life of Charles Blacker Vignoles* (1889), ch. xvi ; *Herapath's Railway and Commercial Journal*, 27 December 1845, p. 2766 ; and the other periodicals cited in the text.

# THE END OF THE GREAT WESTERN
# RAILWAY

To ANY one who loves the West Country, the disappearance
of the Great Western Railway must be a matter for regret.
I do not mean on economic grounds : the case for nationalisation is a strong one, and I am not concerned to discuss
it here. I am simply thinking of the Great Western as one
of the historic institutions of the West Country, and I see
its passing as one more stage towards eliminating all local
differences and establishing instead great impersonal
institutions on a national scale. For more than a hundred
years it played an essential part in the life of the West
Country—fostering agriculture, helping to bring material
comforts and a higher standard of living to many thousands
of people, building up the tourist traffic, the biggest of
modern West-Country industries. And at the same time
it quietly grew into a character itself, its great shadow
lying over the whole West of England : a character for
whom one came to feel a personal affection.

The Great Western Railway is one of the many things
we owe to the city of Bristol. It was there, and not in
London, that it originated. After a good deal of preliminary discussion, the first meeting to found a " Bristol
and London Railroad Company " was held in January
1833. Among the people who attended it were representatives of the city corporation, the Chamber of Com-

merce, the Merchant Venturers, and the Bristol Dock Company. They formed a committee, and one of the first things they did was to appoint an engineer: Isambard Kingdom Brunel. Their choice was a striking act of faith. For Brunel was only twenty-seven at the time, and he was known chiefly as the designer of the Clifton Suspension Bridge—a work barely begun, round which controversy had raged all along. But the trust the committee placed in him was never withdrawn. He remained closely associated with the railway for the rest of his life, and it bears the strong marks of his genius.

By the summer of 1833 a preliminary survey had been completed, a committee had been formed in London corresponding to that in Bristol, and the company's title had been changed to " Great Western Railway ". After some difficulty, powers to construct the line were secured by Act of Parliament in 1835.

The building of a railway nearly 120 miles long was a great undertaking, and it did not go forward very quickly at the start. It was only in the summer of 1838 that the first section of the line, from London to Maidenhead, was opened: the first trains began to run through between London and Bristol three years later. There is a peculiarity in the construction of the railway that is worth mentioning, because it has left traces that are plainly visible to this day. The work was begun simultaneously at both extremities of the line, supervised by two committees, which were largely independent of each other and adopted different policies on some important points. As a result, at the London end all the stations and works were built economically —they were decent, but austere : on the western half of the line, however, a good deal of ornament was provided for, and things were executed with much more flourish.

There was something to be said for both policies, to

my mind, even from a strictly aesthetic point of view. The
plain brick bridge over the Thames at Maidenhead is still
one of the noblest bridges in England, and that at Mouls-
ford further west is not much inferior to it. On the other
hand the works at the Bristol end, many of them carried
out in Bath stone, are quite beautiful : look at the built-
up mouths of the tunnels, or—best of all, perhaps—the
charming ornamental work along the line as you slip into
Bath, skirting Sydney Gardens. All these details—and
there are many more—are worth studying still, the evidence
of a fine architectural tradition applied, naturally and
suitably, to the new needs of the railway.

The Great Western steadily expanded. It built branches
on its own account and worked in close association with a
number of independent companies, which it ultimately
absorbed. Such, for instance, were the Bristol and Exeter
Railway ; the South Devon, which continued the main
line from Exeter to Plymouth ; the Cornwall Railway, from
Plymouth to Falmouth ; and the West Cornwall that ran
from Truro to Penzance. The main line was thus built by
five separate companies, and it did not come fully under the
control of the Great Western till 1876. By that time the
Company had extended in other directions too—into
South Wales and the West Midlands, as far north as Chester
and Birkenhead. It had become the " Great Western "
indeed.

The founders of the Company were a remarkable set
of men. The most famous of them is certainly Brunel. Of
all British railway engineers, I think it is true to say that
Brunel had the most fertile and original mind. He was a
man of astonishing foresight, constantly ahead of his time,
and all his work was touched with imagination. But if he
inherited from his French father a brilliant intellectual
clarity, he had something, too, of the French passion for

logic; and that led him into some great mistakes. He would see the logical superiority of the solution he devised to a problem in engineering and press it forward accordingly against all opposition: he brushed aside with impatience the practical difficulties that might lie in its way. The broad gauge furnishes an obvious example. There is no doubt that if British railways had been built to a seven-foot gauge, and a corresponding height, their operation would now be more economical and efficient. But the question was in fact decided in favour of the narrow gauge at least as early as 1845. Brunel refused to accept the decision. Under his influence the Great Western clung to the broad gauge well into the sixties and seventies: for the extension from Hungerford to Devizes, which was opened in 1862, for instance, for the Thame and Oxford line, and—latest of all—for the St. Ives branch of 1877. But by that time the Great Western had come to recognise that it must eventually fall into line with the rest of the English companies, and a great and costly conversion from the broad to the narrow gauge was taken in hand, which was not completed till 1892. So although I never travel down the Great Western from London to Bristol without being reminded at some point of its creator, I feel we are bound to recognise too the limitations of his soaring, original mind.

Brunel has perhaps received more than his fair share of the credit for making the Great Western Railway. There are other men with strong claims for recognition too: Charles Russell, for example, Tory Member of Parliament for Reading, who was chairman of the Company from 1839 to 1855, ruling and guiding it with admirable firmness; and C. A. Saunders, the first secretary of the Great Western, who served for thirty years as its chief executive officer. Neither Russell nor Saunders finds a place in the *Dictionary of National Biography.* Yet, together with the engineers, Brunel and Daniel Gooch, they were responsible for building up the Company, one of the great institutions of nineteenth-century England. And one further thing is worth noticing about them : the extraordinary youth-fulness of the team. Russell, certainly, was fifty-three when he was elected chairman ; but Saunders became secretary at thirty-seven, Brunel was ten years younger, and—though it sounds incredible—Gooch was appointed locomotive superintendent at the age of twenty. No playing for safety here, choosing middle-aged men of established reputation : that was not the habit of the Early Victorians.

Something of the excitement that these young men felt in making the new railway can still be caught from the reminiscences of Gooch. They show us the novelty of the work, the bold improvisations that had to be made to meet difficulties that had not been looked for. Gooch found that the early engines, which had been ordered before his appointment, were highly unreliable, and he was constantly experimenting with improvements. Brunel and he spent most of Christmas Day in 1838 working in the smith's shop on an alteration to an engine's blast-pipe.[1] There was danger in the life as well. The main line from London to Bristol was completed in 1841 and opened to the public on 30 June. Only one line of rails was finished through the great Box tunnel, and Gooch therefore under-took to travel himself with every train that passed through it, to see that all precautions were taken against accident. After two days of this, about 11 o'clock on the second night, " I was going up the tunnel with the last up train ", he tells us, " when I fancied I saw some green lights placed as they were in front of our trains. A second's reflection convinced me it was the mail coming down.

[1] *Diaries of Sir Daniel Gooch* (1892), 43.

I lost no time in reversing the engine I was on and running back to Box station with my train as quickly as I could, when the mail came down behind me. The policeman at the top of the tunnel had made some blunder and sent the mails on when they arrived there. Had the tunnel not been pretty clear of steam, we must have met in full career, and the smash would have been fearful, cutting short my career also."[1] Like all the men of his class and age, Gooch took hard work for granted. When the railway was opened to Exeter on 1 May 1844 he himself drove the first train down from London and back again. His day began with an inspection of the engine and incidental preparations for the trip ; the train left at 7.30 and reached Exeter in five hours ; there he had business to attend to all the time, except during an hour given to dinner ; at 5.20 he started back again ; the train rolled into Paddington at 10. He had driven it 390 miles. He records the bare time-table in his diary and adds only this modest comment : " Next day my back ached so much I could hardly walk. Mr. Brunel wrote me a very handsome letter, thanking me for what I had done, and all were very much pleased."[2]

They had good reason to be pleased. The company that Gooch and Brunel and their associates built up became a prosperous and comfortable corporation, disputing with the London and North-Western the primacy among the old British railway companies. It was not, indeed, all plain sailing. In the forties the Great Western made a splendid display : the broad gauge was on trial for its life, and its protagonists were out to show what it could do. The Great Western may fairly claim to have run the first express trains in the world. In 1847 it became possible to reach Bristol from London in 2 hours 35 minutes. The first stage of the

[1] ibid., 49-50.
[2] ibid., 52-3.

journey, the 53 miles to Didcot, was covered in 55 minutes. For more than four years (December 1847–March 1852) those times were maintained. Then they were suddenly abandoned, and from 1853 onwards it took 68 minutes to reach Didcot by the best train, and 3 hours 15 minutes to Bristol. A need for economy seems to have caused this set-back. No doubt the Great Western directors felt there was no call for such speeds, which were greater than those any other railway could show. Having demonstrated their effortless superiority, they sat back and dozed off to sleep.

They not only dozed : they began to snore. The sixties were a troubled age in railway politics, and the Great Western did not master its difficulties then with the triumphant ease of the forties. Instead, it became a byword for caution, for conservatism, and—to the public—for inconvenience. A pushing concern like the Midland might show dangerous democratic tendencies, carrying third-class passengers on all its trains from 1872, abolishing second class outright in 1875, and claiming, with disgusting impudence, that these measures effected economies and brought in an increased revenue. The Great Western stuck to its old aristocratic policy with rigour. Not until 1869 were third-class passengers admitted to a single train on the system that could by any stretch of imagination be called fast. That was a major concession ; and it was thirteen more years before the third-class passenger got another from the Great Western.

By the eighties the company had a generally bad name, as a great body that had sunk down into the lethargy of repletion. This ill repute was not entirely deserved. It was in 1872, at a time of apparent torpor, that the Great Western undertook the stupendous work of building the Severn Tunnel, to give a better route from London to South Wales and from Bristol to the North. It took fourteen years to complete the tunnel, which, with seven miles of new line, cost nearly £2,000,000. The investment was a long-term one ; but it was shrewd, and in the end it paid.

To the general public, however, such works did not mean very much. What they wanted was better service, and that was a long time in coming. Foxwell summed up the Great Western's reputation very well in 1889 : " It is in many ways such a great line that its meanness in the matter of quick trains is the more incongruous ; thus twenty years ago its Exeter expresses ran at the same speed as now . . . The Great Western is a very solid line, and makes its progress in a stolid style : doing some great things and many small, but all alike with the immovability of Jove."[1]

By the time those words were published a change had already begun. It can be dated precisely, in July 1888, with the appointment of N. J. Burlinson as Superintendent of the Line.[2] During the next quarter of a century the whole face of the Great Western altered. It drew ahead to regain the supremacy that it had held in the forties, until the " Cornish Riviera Express ", on its introduction in 1904, began to run non-stop between London and Plymouth—easily the longest non-stop journey in the world, made at an average speed of 55 miles an hour. Comparable improvements took place on the other Great Western main routes, and they were helped by the building of a number of short cuts, which knocked twenty miles off the distance to Plymouth and nineteen off that to Birmingham. The Company's detractors used to maintain that the initials " G.W.R. " stood for " Great Way Round ". Now they could no longer use that gibe.

The improvement thus begun at the end of the eighties

[1] E. Foxwell and T. C. Farrer, *Express Trains, English and Foreign* (1889), 27.
[2] E. T. MacDermot, *History of the Great Western Railway* (1927-1931), ii. 399.

was steadily maintained. Like all the other British railways, the Great Western went through a difficult time in the first World War. But it emerged strong and resilient; and the Railways Act of 1921 faced it with an easier task than any of its fellows. For they were all called upon to group themselves with neighbouring companies to form larger units, more economic to run in the changed conditions of the twentieth century. The London and South Western— to take the Great Western's nearest rival as an example— had to accommodate itself to working with the London, Brighton and South Coast and the South Eastern and Chatham in a new Southern Railway; and that adjustment inevitably took time and brought special problems with it. But the Great Western was so big a company in its own right, and so physically compact, that it was merely required to absorb the small South Wales lines and one or two others of minor importance. In effect it remained unaltered. And so when, on 31 December 1922, the old historic names disappeared—London and North Western, Midland, North Eastern, Great Northern, and the others—the Great Western alone lived on.

It had exactly twenty-five more years of life, and they were of a piece with its previous history. The service it afforded improved further, in almost every respect. In the 1930s its express trains were better than they had ever been before—and better than they ever seem likely to be again.[1] That is a simple test of comparison, which has naturally been used all through this essay to indicate the facilities the company offered to the public and its consequent reputation. But there are many others that could be made. The Great Western, alone among the British railways, introduced a system of automatic train control, which contributed much to maintaining its high record of

[1] See Appendix, pp. 246-9

safety : there was not a single serious accident on the line between 1904 and 1936. Again, it would be no more than a statement of fact to say that the design of its locomotives throughout the first thirty years of this century influenced that of all other British companies, and in some ways set them an example.

Yet here, once more, we can see that the old character of the Great Western persisted. In the 1930s all the other companies went in for streamlined locomotives. The Great Western made two half-hearted little experiments in that direction and then dropped the idea altogether. It never embarked on special high-speed express trains, like the London and North Eastern's " Coronation ". You can hear the Great Western's comment almost as if it had been spoken aloud. Such fancy stunts were too much like tricks at a circus ; these trains could not truly pay their way ; the revenue they brought in could never compensate adequately for the dislocation of all other traffic that they caused.

There is no need to discuss the merits and demerits of those contentions. Here it is enough to note that the Great Western put no faith in such spectacular expedients. By now it represented the sturdiest conservative tradition among the British railway companies : not one of deliberately staying put, still less one of reaction ; but a careful consolidation, an ordered development along established lines.

That was apparent to the ordinary traveller, in a multitude of little ways. No other company preserved so rigid a distinction between first and third-class passengers. There was nothing offensive about it : if you travelled third you were well looked after. But there always remained an opulence about a Great Western first-class carriage that was striking in comparison with the austerer, less roomy accommodation offered in a third. And why not? Why grade up the third, as the northern lines did, so that it is practically indistinguishable from the first? Abolish all passenger class distinctions if you like—there is something to be said for it, though by no means everything : but if you keep them, surely it is only sensible to see that there really are some plain advantages left to the first-class traveller?

The Great Western had its almost human oddities, certain features that persisted through many years of its life and made it different from all its rivals. The extraordinary length of time its trains stopped at stations, for example. When they were running, they ran very fast— for many years the Great Western held a number of the world's speed records ; but when they stopped, it often seemed as if they had stopped for ever. A train might call at Crewe or at York for two minutes : no train ever spent less than five at a Great Western station of any size, and its stop would often be for ten minutes or a quarter of an hour. Things were done here with dignity ; the luggage and the mail-bags were put in and out, the passengers shepherded into the trains, the doors shut, the whistles blown—all with the majesty of an immemorial routine. (One thinks again of Foxwell's phrase about " the immovability of Jove ".)

It had a pleasant and soothing effect. You travelled on the Great Western in comfort : even in the pinched and harassing 1940s it would sometimes give you the curious illusion that you were really living in 1910. On the remoter branch lines you were sometimes transported back much further still. I can well remember, some fifteen years ago, travelling on one of them in an ancient four-wheeled coach. In my compartment there was a notice, dated in the nineties, stating that " bottles of claret, price one shilling ",

MAIDENHEAD BRIDGE, GREAT WESTERN RAILWAY

From a lithograph in J. C. Bourne's *History and Description of the Great Western Railway* (1846)

Entrance of the Great Western Railway through Sydney Gardens
into Bath

From a lithograph in J. C. Bourne's *History and Description
of the Great Western Railway* (1846)

might be obtained from the guard (or the stationmaster, I forget which). It was, alas, only a notice. The bottles of claret have gone the way of all the other paraphernalia of Victorian travel—the luncheon-baskets, the foot-warmers, the travelling caps and rugs, the oil lamps, the yellow railway novels.

What a character those Great Western branches had! The line down to Fowey that Q loved ; the extraordinary antics of the train going to Looe ; the bleak Princetown railway—I can hear the grinding of the wheels round its sharp curves now ; the Cheddar Valley line with its spiky Gothic stations. Here, if anywhere, one could still savour the life of an earlier world. Or think, again, of the Fairford branch, running gently down into East Gloucestershire. It was long used as a repository for venerable, even historic engines—its duties, I suppose, are the easiest that an engine could be asked to perform. The line was built in the seventies, with extreme economy : when it comes to a hill it mounts, like a road, and descends the other side, for cuttings are expensive. In bad weather (the thaw of March 1947, for instance) there is a great water-splash under every bridge, through which the train flounders. So the line goes on to the west, until it ends near Fairford— abruptly, in the middle of a field. You can think of it as William Morris's railway, for it serves the country of *News from Nowhere* : it seems almost to be part of the book.

The Great Western, alone among English railways, has cut some figure in literature. Remember the opening of *Zuleika Dobson*, the scene on the station at Oxford that " whispers the last enchantment of the Middle Age " ; and Thomas Hardy's poem, " Midnight on the Great Western " :

> *In the third-class seat sat the journeying boy,*
> *And the roof-lamp's oily flame*

*Played down on his listless form and face,*
*Bewrapt past knowing to what he was going,*
*Or whence he came.*

*In the band of his hat the journeying boy*
*Had a ticket stuck ; and a string*
*Around his neck bore the key of his box,*
*That twinkled gleams of the lamp's sad beams*
*Like a living thing . . .*

The Great Western turns up time and time again: in
Richard Jefferies and Edward Thomas, in the journal of
Arnold Bennett, in Bradley's *Exmoor Memories* and Saints-
bury's *Scrap Books*—not to mention Turner's " Rain,
Steam, and Speed ", one of the finest pictures of his last
period.[1]

I think this is all evidence of the strong impression the
Great Western made on people's minds. And indeed if
you travelled much on the railway you could hardly escape
it. You constantly felt that this was a powerful corporation
with a long history behind it : in the air of its great
stations, Paddington and Temple Meads and Snow Hill
at Birmingham, and the lordly way its lines were laid out
—look at the ample, sweeping embankments as the train
runs down through Somerton. And however little you
were interested in railways, you could not fail to notice
the names of the Great Western's engines, especially
in earlier days when their brass name-plates were always
kept brightly polished. It was not merely the names of
places you knew and loved—*Restormel Castle* or *Tintern
Abbey*. There was so much history here, too. The wars,
for example, left their mark on the Great Western's engines :
*Eupatoria, Sebastopol, Inkerman* ; *Atbara, Mafeking* ; and

---

[1] For the story that lies behind that picture see a letter from Mrs. John Simon to
Ruskin, printed in *Praeterita* (Hart-Davis, 1949), 574-8.

then in our own time, admirably maintaining the tradition, *Thunderbolt, Hurricane, Spitfire.*

The debt that the West Country owes to its great railway is very heavy. In building up its industries : the market-gardening of West Cornwall and the Scilly Islands, to take a single example out of many. That is dependent on the railway, in fact its creation ; for nothing but a railway can transport the flowers and early vegetables so quickly and in such bulk to London. But the most striking of all the Great Western's services to the West of England has been its development of the tourist traffic. A century ago, before the railway was built, Torquay was a small watering-place and Cornwall a remote, half-foreign land, to be explored only by the adventurous. The Great Western Railway has altered all that. It has made the south-western counties the great holiday country of England : it has wrought a complete change in their economy—you might well call it a new " industrial revolution ".

In the century of its prosperous and useful life the Great Western made its own contribution to English history. The mark it has left on the West Country is too strong to be wiped out ; and when the green engines, with their copper and brass work, and the yellow and brown paint have disappeared, I hope the Great Western will not be forgotten.

# MY FIRST ACQUAINTANCE WITH
# SCOTLAND

I AM an Englishman. I had a Scots great-grandmother, and there is Anglo-Irish blood on my mother's side ; but I am not aware that these strains have meant much to me. All my roots lie in England : my tastes are English, and so, I suppose, are the prejudices of my mind. More than that, I am a Southerner—by conviction as well as by birth. I have visited the North of England a good deal, and I am much attached to the North-West, particularly to Westmorland and the country round Carlisle. But even there I feel I am among strangers : much more so in Yorkshire or Durham.

In the course of the last twenty years I have travelled all over England. I think I can claim to have a fair working knowledge of the country as a whole, with a few important exceptions—Shropshire, industrial Lancashire, the extreme North-East. I also know South Wales quite well. But, alas, I have not seen Ireland ; and it is not long since I crossed the Border into Scotland for the first time. More than once in earlier years I looked out across the Debatable Lands from Carlisle, from Brampton and Naworth to the hills above Liddesdale, over the Solway to Criffell : but I never ventured further than that. My business lay south of the Border, and (I may as well confess it at once) I was on the whole content that it should be so. For I fear I am somewhat insensitive to many of the things Scotland stands for. The Highlands give me no twinge of romance. I am not merely bored by Jacobitism : I regard it with distaste, as an obstruction and a nuisance. I have little sympathy for Mary, Queen of Scots—though some for James I, whom Scotsmen usually regard less warmly. Indeed Scottish political history, as far as I have read it, seems to me a dismal story, a catalogue of brutality, treachery, and squalor. It becomes interesting to me only when Scotland loses her independence at the Union, with the splendid flowering of Edinburgh and Glasgow in the eighteenth and nineteenth centuries. An Englishman's view, once again, for which I make apology to Scotsmen : but I have to set it down at the outset in order to show the state of mind, clear and definite, in which I first crossed the Border.

Now that I have said these things in depreciation of Scotland, I must add at once that two of the men I admire above all others were Scots : Walter Scott and David Livingstone. It was they alone who drew me strongly to their country, and especially to the two great towns with which they were associated. I hope to write of Scott one day : but I was actually writing of Livingstone when I made this journey, and so, on my first visit, it was he who dominated my mind.

When the train left St. Pancras, I felt I was bound on an adventure, and the prospect excited me. I had one companion in my carriage, an elderly lady with a soft Scots voice, and we soon fell into conversation. I confided in her that I was on my first visit to her country. She asked me where I was going, and when I said, " To Glasgow ", she replied, " Oh, but I hope you're going further than that ", and went on to tell me that Glasgow was no place to visit—fearful lest I should think it was characteristic of Scotland. I assured her that I was much looking forward to the experience, that I had some idea of what Glasgow was like and was particularly interested in its history. This put a damper on the conversation: obviously thinking that the English were a queer lot, she retired into a Dorothy Sayers.

The train ran on through the pleasant East Midlands and the less pleasant industrial country of Derbyshire and the West Riding. At Leeds all the people who had joined us on the way got out. They were replaced by two tough little Scots boys and their placid mother: they bounced and scrambled in and out of the compartment, exclaiming shrill, unintelligible things, for four and a half hours, till at last they got out at Kilmarnock.

For many years past I had wanted to travel from Leeds to Carlisle. It is obvious from a glance at the map that it must be a splendid journey. In fact, I found it more than that: it is, to my mind beyond question, the most magnificent railway journey in England. On the main West Coast line you have, it is true, five wonderful minutes as you skirt Morecambe Bay and look over Lancaster Sands to the mountains of the Lake District, drawn up in their great ranks. But after that, though the mountains are still there, on both sides of you, they seem to lose shape, to become no more than a shifting panorama of masses tumbled carelessly together. The crossing of the Pennines, on the other hand, is ordered like some great play. First the gentle ascent of Airedale, past Keighley (the Brontës' train waiting at the platform) to Skipton. Then the long climb over the saddle between Pen-y-ghent and Ingleborough, across the grim waste beyond, glancing from the watershed at the streams that run off it to form the rivers of Lancashire and Yorkshire—Ribble and Lune and Ure; and so down into the exquisite valley of the Eden for the last act of the play.

I have never been so much moved by a railway journey. The architecture of the mountains is unforgettable, Ingleborough and Whernside above all. The names, too: as the train raced on they formed themselves to fit its rhythm:

*Batty Moss and Mallerstang*
*Ribblehead and Dent.*

And over it all one spirit presided, the indomitable spirit of Anne Clifford, Countess of Dorset, Pembroke, and Montgomery, who travelled this way so often in the seventeenth century and has left her mark on the country ever since in the castles she occupied. One after another the train runs by them: Skipton, Pendragon, Appleby— the ears of its Norman keep pricked up above the little town, the rooks circling round it in the evening.

As the play went on I could do nothing but sit with my eyes to the window, taking notes. I longed for some one to watch it with me. Overcome by it all at one point, I exclaimed at its splendour to the old Scots lady opposite, who happened to look up from her novel just then. I got no response. She volunteered only one remark of her own accord. As we were running into Carlisle we passed some geese in a field. She looked at me, highly pleased, said "Christmas dinner", and returned to read once more. "A Philistine people", I thought to myself with scorn: "no sense of beauty, nothing but materialists. I always knew they were like that."

But I was wrong. I had done the old lady, and her people, an injustice. At the very moment of crossing the Border at Gretna, as the train ran over the little bridge, she closed her Dorothy Sayers with a snap and began to fix her attention on the fields outside. Then I knew what she felt. She felt as I do when I am travelling back from the Midlands to Oxford and first see the Cherwell at

Banbury, with its fringe of pollard willows.  No more reading for me then : I am in the South, coming home. I know Cornishmen, too, who habitually ignore the Quantocks and Exeter and Powderham, the sea at Dawlish and the distant skyline of Dartmoor : but directly the train begins to rumble over the Saltash bridge, they too shut their books, with the same snap of contentment.  So I understood the old lady, and felt drawn to her with a much greater warmth.

She talked to me about the Solway—that mysterious waste of sand and grey water, filled always with the memory of *Redgauntlet*. We went on to speak of Criffell ; and then she began to gather up her belongings, put on a handsome tweed cloak, bade me a pleasant time in Scotland, and got out of the train at Dumfries.

It was past six o'clock.  As we climbed up Nithsdale the mountains closed in on us in the gathering dusk.  It was no use to look out for Drumlanrig, as I had been told to do : nothing for it but to concentrate on a good dinner. I returned to my compartment to find the small boys subdued at last, buttoned up in thick black mackintoshes and sou'-westers, waiting to get out at Kilmarnock.  Their departure left me with two companions, who had been asleep but now woke up and started an animated conversation, of which I could understand hardly anything at first. One was clearly a Highlander, a little dark ugly man, full of life and humour, his whole conversation a dramatic show of gesture and grimace.  The other I took for a Lowlander : tall, handsome, fair, and slower of speech, though he too was enjoying himself.  I wished they would say something intelligible.  Presently they did—or at least I began to get used to their voices and to pick up some words here and there.  Then the Highlander, seeing I was reading a guide-book to Scotland, asked me if I was coming up for a holiday.  I said no, that I was going to Glasgow only for a very short visit on business.  At once he began to tell me all the things I should do and see in Glasgow, regardless of my protests that I should have very little free time.  There was the People's Palace : there were also the shipyards, and the Firth of Clyde.  (I could get to Rothesay and back, he told me, for 5s. 3d.)  The Lowlander then chipped in to ask me if I had come from London. I said I had, whereupon he gave a charming, rather bashful grin, and told me that I should find Glasgow very slow after that.  But he went on, with a little encouragement from me, to say that he preferred the slowness : London was too fast for him.  It was only a step from this to something that I knew would turn up soon : the excellence of the Glasgow trams, and their cheapness.  This is usually the first thing I am told about Glasgow : I was only surprised that the subject took at least a quarter of an hour to appear on this occasion.  However, I was then carefully instructed in the principles of catching trams and in the iniquitous conduct of the present manager of the city's transport, who had not only muddled all the trams up together instead of keeping them confined to certain routes, according to the colours in which they were painted, but—even worse—had raised the maximum fare from $2\frac{1}{2}$d. to 4d.

We were now running into Glasgow.  The Highlander took care to show me the Gorbals, especially one of the old tenements, with a dim light burning in a window. Even in the darkness, I agreed, it looked sufficiently grim. Further instructions about places I must visit crowded in on me.  He insisted on presenting me with his pocket railway time-table—a touching present, which I shall keep. He also inquired closely if I had arranged where I was going to stay.  When I assured him I had and the train entered St. Enoch station, he and his companion left me, once again with the kindest good wishes for my visit to Scotland.

I was a little overpowered by all this. It had been a strain to keep up with the conversation, in this half-foreign language—I cannot pretend I understood more than two words in three : all I could do was to try and disguise my lack of comprehension. And I had another feeling besides, an obscure feeling of shame. Suppose it had been the other way round. Would those two have met with a welcome on their way to London like theirs to me as we drew towards Glasgow ? And would they have been told half as much by Englishmen of what they should do in London, or half so intelligently ? I am compelled to answer " no " to both questions.

From these two encounters in the train, then, I arrived at Glasgow with a grateful sense of welcome. As soon as I had claimed my room at the hotel and cleaned myself up after the journey, I felt I must go out and explore, even though in darkness. There was a keen wind blowing : it was much colder than in England, and I was glad of my overcoat. The people of Glasgow seemed to think the same, for they stood in doorways, shuffling from one foot to the other to keep themselves warm. I walked down first of all to look at the Clyde. There is something that always fascinates me about a river at night, the oily quality of its waters, their intense blackness. Here they were even more impressive than usual. For I have never been in such a dark town as Glasgow. In the course of a leisurely re-reading of the Waverley Novels, I happened just at this time (appropriately, but by accident) to have reached *Rob Roy*, one of my special favourites. Francis Osbaldistone describes the streets of Glasgow tersely as " dark, uneven, and ill-paved ". Those words apply exactly to them still.

The street-lighting is miserable, and the pavements seem to have been constructed from slabs of granite, large and small, broken and whole, some of them tilted at an angle of twenty or thirty degrees. Walking along them even in dry weather is therefore most uncomfortable; women, with their thin shoes, must find it agonising; and when it rains, every one's shoes and stockings are filthy.

Next morning I went up first to see the cathedral, thinking I might not have another chance over the week-end and being determined not to miss it. I had read a good deal about it beforehand in the histories of architecture, and the account of it in *Rob Roy* was fresh in my mind, so that I was prepared for a building unlike any other I had ever seen. But I found it more remarkable even than I had expected. To begin with, its extraordinary situation and surroundings took me completely by surprise. I knew it stood on a steep slope, which allowed the construction of its famous crypt. What I knew nothing of was the Necropolis on the hill beyond. It looked like something in a dream (or rather a nightmare), the skyline serrated with the edges of the monuments, like a ghastly Golgotha in some sixteenth-century German painting: terrible, impressive, above all—in the literal sense of the word—incredible.

I had no time then to inspect the Necropolis closely. My business was with the interior of the cathedral. There I found nothing to startle me, though the strength and loftiness of the design were altogether greater than I had anticipated, and the crypt far darker, more sinister and exciting. I understood now how easily Rob Roy could hide behind his pillar to whisper into Francis Osbaldistone's ear and then, his message delivered, glide away through the crypt " like the spectre of one of the numerous dead who rested within its precincts "

Glasgow cathedral, then, is something more than the grandest church in Scotland. The fury of the Reformation destroyed all its close competitors—and there were never many of them : so that is a somewhat empty compliment. It should be said rather that it is a very remarkable church in its own right, with a quality and atmosphere as powerful, and as peculiar, as those of Ely or Durham.

I had now to hurry back to catch a bus for Blantyre, the village in which Livingstone was born. It lies up the valley of the Clyde, half-a-dozen miles east of Glasgow, on the edge of the Lanarkshire coal-field. Its drab main street reminded me of many in South Wales—the poor little grey stone buildings with their slate roofs, the colliery-wheels in the distance. And, to make the resemblance stronger, it started to drizzle. I walked down through a trim little park, past the station and a group of pre-fabricated army huts, now occupied by civilian families and cheerful with gardens and children. In front lay a bank of trees, and the Clyde in a hidden valley below them. A high red sandstone wall, a sharp turn to the left, and there was the building in which Livingstone was born, now preserved as a Scottish National Memorial to his memory.

It was my good fortune to be shown over it by Dr. Macnair, the creator of the Memorial and the chairman of the Trust that controls it. Again I found something very much bigger and more impressive than I had expected. I knew a little of the Memorial before, and particularly of its Livingstone manuscripts, which were the things I had come mainly to see. But I had no idea of the extent of its collection of relics, their intimate character, or their vital importance for an understanding of Livingstone's life.

To begin with the building. It is in two parts : a tall three-storied block with two external stair-turrets, of a fashion characteristic of Scotland; and a lower block of two stories, the upper reached by little curved flights of stone steps, guarded by iron railings. It was in the tall building that Livingstone was born. In the ground floor of the small block he learnt his A B C. The two blocks together form the " Shuttle Row ". They were built about 1785 to house the weavers in the great cotton mill that stood just below, down by the river bank. (It has now almost wholly disappeared.) The tall block was divided up into twenty-four rooms, each one occupied by a complete family.

The room in which Livingstone was born in 1813 is on the top floor, looking down to the river and across to the woods of Bothwell, which must still be very much as they were when he knew them. It is a situation of astonishing beauty. The woods are thick with bluebells in spring : when I saw them the trees were just turning, tawny and yellow and pale green with the onset of autumn. Livingstone had a hard life of it at Blantyre, working in the mill from the age of ten ; but the image of the Clyde bit deep into his mind, and more than once on his travels in Africa he turned for a likeness to the country he had known as a boy.

The room itself, like its fellows, measures ten feet by fourteen. It is fitted with two beds, built into recesses in the wall, a little kitchen range, and two cupboards. Some of the furniture it now contains was in the room in Livingstone's childhood : the old clock, for instance, with its noisy, cheerful tick and long pendulum, known as " the Wag at the Wa' ". Outside, in a case, hangs the lovely Paisley shawl in which the child was carried to Blantyre church to be baptised.

As you work your way through the rooms of the Shuttle Row you are conducted through Livingstone's life. Considering that he spent almost all of it in Africa it is remarkable that so many relics of him should have been preserved. I agree with Dr. Macnair that it can be accounted for only in one way : by the unique impression he made on every one he met, Europeans and Africans alike. They kept the most trifling things that had belonged to him and guarded them as treasures. More striking still, when the Memorial was founded twenty years ago the owners of these things gave them up, crowding in to present them ; and with very few exceptions they were adamant in refusing all payment for the things they offered. I know of no other museum built up in quite this way, and I have never seen one that touched me more deeply. Indeed I know only two that can compare with it—Dove Cottage and the room at Dorchester that contains the relics of Thomas Hardy.

The things that move one most at Blantyre—I suppose it is inevitable—are those that are associated with Livingstone's last journey, that unbelievable record of endurance and faith ; and two, perhaps, above all. First his pocket Testament, read and re-read in those years : he recorded himself that he read through the whole Bible four times while he was in the Manyuema country alone, between 1869 and 1871. The passages he returned to most frequently can be found from the marks of his thumbs on the pages. It lies open now at one of them—the twenty-third Psalm, in a metrical version. No wonder he loved it so much. It fitted his own circumstances exactly :

> *Yea, though I walk in death's dark vale,*
> *yet will I fear none ill :*
> *For thou art with me ; and thy rod*
> *and staff me comfort still.*

And then—the most precious thing of all—the little

pocket notebook in which he kept up his journal in the last days of his life, and the blunt stump of pencil with which he wrote it. No facsimile or description can convey the impression it makes : the clear, firm, familiar hand, the relentless quest for the information he is seeking—his very last words are given to noting the name of the river along whose banks he is being carried.

Besides these relics, the Memorial also contains a number of maps, models, imaginative reconstructions of scenes from Livingstone's life. The student of his work may perhaps regret for a moment this mingling of fiction with history. Yet it too has its place, and one could not possibly wish it away. For it is by means of these things that the Memorial succeeds in interesting children. They come here in their thousands in the summer, brought in school parties from all over western Scotland. Dr. Macnair told me that there are sometimes 3,000 of them on a fine Saturday afternoon. The Trust owns a field of nine acres beside the Shuttle Row, where they can play and picnic. To an Englishman—to me—it sounded at first very strange : it tempted me to a cynical thought about sugaring the pill of education. But then, as I worked round the Memorial myself in the course of the day, I listened to the comments of some children who happened to be there, and I found that it held their attention : more, that it filled their minds. And it made me realise, as I had not realised before, the great gulf between England and Scotland. Nothing like the Livingstone Memorial exists in England. If it did, it would never be a centre of real interest to children in this way. To think of drawing 50,000 people a year to see a museum devoted to a missionary—the idea is preposterous in the England of the nineteen-fifties. But it is not preposterous in Scotland. It is a simple accomplished fact. The reasons are plain to

see : the more serious character of Scottish education, and
the greater hold that Christianity still has over the Scottish
mind.  I do not share that religious belief ; but I feel much
more confidence in the value of the school education the
Scots base upon it—narrow and dry though at some points
it may be—than in most of the flabby experiments we are
now engaged on in England.

By the time I got back into Glasgow from Blantyre it
was nearly dark.  The rain had kindly paused while I was
looking at the outside of the Memorial, and its surroundings.  But during the afternoon it came on in earnest, and
it scarcely stopped before I left Glasgow.  I had intended,
as a necessary part of my visit, to make the trip down the
Clyde, past the shipyards and out into the Firth.  But the
weather next day was too dismal, and I abandoned the
attempt.  Instead, I bent my way back to the cathedral.
Being Sunday, and between the hours of service, it
was impossible to get in—even the outside gate of the
churchyard was locked.  So I devoted myself to the exterior
this time.  I shall never forget looking up at it from below
on that wet afternoon : crypt and quire together, the great
black wall towered above me like a cliff of basalt.  It also
began to take on new virtues as a building, the more closely
I studied it from the south-east.  The complicated pro-
portions of its tiers are admirably disposed ; the shallow
transepts lead your eye up to the stumpy spire with
a brutal and fitting abruptness ; the contrast in colour is
excellent—the blackness of the walls set off by the pale
green copper of the roof, shining under the rain.  No
photograph I have seen of the cathedral has given the
least idea of its majesty, when seen from this side.

That led me to reflect again—the thought had occurred
to me before—how very little Glasgow has done to pro-
claim itself to the world.  Here is a city of a most powerful

RICHARD LANDER
From a drawing by William Brockedon (1831)
in the National Portrait Gallery

RICHARD LANDER
From a painting by William Brockedon
in the Colonial Office

character; on a splendid site, the two little rivers cutting their step gullies down to the Clyde; its docks and ship-yards among the greatest in the world; the modern city growing out of an interesting past, of which some fine memorials remain. Yet the stranger, arriving in Glasgow unprepared, is left to discover all this for himself. I could not find even the simplest guide to the town, apart from a tram and bus map, useful but rather impersonal. I wondered why it was. This is all too common in England : not many of our great towns do much to make the visitor aware of the remarkable things they have to show. But here I expected something different. Glasgow is bigger than any of the English provincial towns ; and I had hoped that the Scots, a better educated people than the English, would have insisted on some intelligent description, in however simple a form, of the things worth seeing and knowing in this great city.

But another thought crossed my mind also. Could it be that the proximity of Edinburgh had damped something of Glasgow's pride in itself? Here I know I am on very dangerous ground. Before ever I arrived, I had been treated to an eloquent and withering account of the wretched inferiority of Edinburgh by my Highland friend in the train—tinged, plainly enough, with an envy of which he was quite unaware. The rivalry between the two cities is well known to every one. Edinburgh has, I take it, certain clear advantages : its past, its streets and buildings, are immeasurably more splendid, its site the most dramatic in the whole of Great Britain. But that is not everything there is to be said. Glasgow, as anybody can see, has a character all its own—utterly different from Edinburgh's, reflecting in that its history. A great pity that it should be so unsuitably modest about itself.

P.E.                                                              N

A ready parallel to this rivalry sprang to my Southerner's mind : I thought of the two cities of Bath and Bristol. The beauty of Bath is as famous in England as the beauty of Edinburgh in Scotland : Bristol, like Glasgow, is a great industrial town developing from an ancient past. The two are even closer together than Edinburgh and Glasgow, a bare ten miles apart. There is a rivalry between them, and occasional bad feeling. Yet Bath, for all its fame, has certainly not snuffed out Bristol's pride in its own history : indeed I think each often stimulates the other by its example. At any rate, Bristol is not only the most interesting of all the great towns of England outside London : it is also one of those with the keenest sense of its past. Could not Glasgow bring itself to learn something from Bristol ?

All the time, with thoughts like these, I was walking through the rain up the winding paths of the Necropolis, past the decent memorials of the merchants of Glasgow, marvelling occasionally at a great Grecian mausoleum hewn in the hillside, noting one or two people from other worlds—a minor Scots poet, a sculptor, young men killed at Gallipoli and Loos. At last I reached the top, to read the inscription on the base of that column that honours John Knox and crowns the whole great hill. Again I found it difficult to believe the sight that lay below me : the grotesque scene of mortality, the ravine and the cathedral beyond, and beyond that the black houses receding through the haze out of sight.

I found the atmosphere of Glasgow fascinating. I have never seen the same quality in the light anywhere else. The rain fell steadily for about thirty-six hours. No, " fell " is the wrong word : to be more accurate, the rain seemed just to descend, throwing a fine film over the whole town. Behind it, all that Sunday afternoon as I trudged round the cathedral and the Necropolis and then across to the university, the sun was shining. It was a dim yellow sun, and it seemed infinitely distant. But, with the rain, it produced a strange luminous glow that hung everywhere, softening the intense blackness of the streets. It might have been a trick peculiar to that afternoon. But I had already noticed something of the same light in the morning, looking down the Clyde from one of the bridges, before it had begun to rain; and I seemed to detect it somewhere else too, in the pictures of Sir D. Y. Cameron. No wonder that there should have been a " Glasgow School " : it is easy to see what inspiration the place must hold for a painter.

I hope it will not seem that I am romanticising Glasgow. It would be impossible for anybody to spend an hour there without becoming aware of the misery—the terror, even —that surrounds and underlies its mercantile grandeur. For my part, I cannot forget it. I have never been in a town where the children played so freely in the streets : not merely those they lived in, but the great main streets with the trams and the shops. At night, for all the rain, I went out to look at the life of the city, once in the western part towards Clydebank, and once round the eastern end of Argyle Street. I saw then something of the poverty and wretchedness in which most of the people of Glasgow live. There was no warmth or geniality here, such as one will sometimes find in an English slum. The very cheekiness of the *gamins* had a kind of desperate ferocity about it. I noticed that the pubs shut at nine ; and the emergence of the crowd at closing-time seemed very different from the noisy good cheer one is accustomed to in England. No doubt I missed the undercurrents, being a foreigner, and the people were less grim than they seemed. But there is no mistaking their general tone. One does not need a social worker or a statistician to tell one that here are some of the worst slums in Western Europe.

What a city this is! It has only one counterpart in England—Liverpool. There you find something of the same violent contrast between wealth and poverty; the same lofty jet-black buildings; the same sense of a vast outer world opening from the Mersey as from the Clyde. But Glasgow has something more as well: it has a metropolitan air about it. That is not a mere matter of population. Birmingham and Manchester-with-Salford are almost as large: yet their atmosphere is utterly different. Nobody, entering either of them, could suppose that he was in a capital city. The huddled, crooked streets betray them both for what they are: overgrown small towns, which sprang up like mushrooms in the nineteenth century. And much of the same small-town spirit has always dominated their minds. Glasgow, on the other hand, has achieved a grandeur that is denied to them: spread out loosely, spaciously, along the low ridge to the north of the Clyde, its streets long and straight, laid out on a grid pattern that artfully avoids monotony. The spirit of the place is acrid, harsh and sombre. Yet it has a real splendour of its own; and I, at any rate, could not help feeling that in Glasgow I was in one of the great cities of the world.

At last, on the Sunday night, I made my way back to my hotel. I went reluctantly, lingering in George Square to look once more at its formidable Municipal Buildings, the statues under the lights, and high above on his column, rightly dominating his countrymen below, the figure of Walter Scott.

Next morning it was time to leave. The rain had stopped. It was a frosty October day, the air very crisp as we pulled out of St. Enoch station. In five minutes we were in the country—and very pleasant country at that, broken, well wooded and ploughed.  A small town or two, and we were in the country again, with the Firth of Clyde in the distance : in half an hour, Kilmarnock.  The railway runs right through Burns's country, but I am sorry to say that this did not stir me much.  I hope I may succeed in reading Burns one day : for the present I fear he means little to me.  I was far more excited at passing Auchinleck, looking over to the woods of the House where Boswell was born and seeing the church by which he is buried.  Perhaps it is characteristic of the Scots that they should make so little of him, and so much of Burns.  Both of them great Romantic figures : but though Burns's life lays itself open to sentimental interpretation, that will not do for Boswell at all.  Another few miles, and another contrast : the little town of Sanquhar, headquarters of the Cameronians in the Killing Time, neat and quiet enough now, with its dark memories of persecution and savage reprisal.  We climbed up through the hills, high above the Nith, shadowed with lovely autumn woods : over the top, and there was Drumlanrig away on the right as we sped easily down to Dumfries.

A different memory now held me.  It was at Thornhill, on this last descent, that Joseph Thomson was born, one of the most intrepid of the explorers of Kenya ; and Annan, the last place we stopped at in Scotland, produced Hugh Clapperton, who made two historic journeys in West Africa.  Over the hills to the east, not very far away, Mungo Park was born : he practised as a surgeon at Peebles in the interval between his two expeditions to the Niger.  What was there in the Scottish Lowlands that made so many great explorers ?  And what impulse drove those three to Africa—for none of them was a missionary, like Livingstone ?  Perhaps there is no answer to these questions.  But this much at least can be said : it was

from Scotland that their tenacity and endurance came,
their clear common sense, and one other quality too—
their ability to understand and deal straightly with Africans,
simple people not altogether unlike those they had known
here at home.

These were the thoughts that passed through my mind
as the train ran along by the Solway out of Scotland. A few
minutes more, and we were leaving Carlisle. I settled back
into my corner to watch once again the superb unfolding
of the Pennines.

# RICHARD LANDER AND THE NIGER

RICHARD LANDER is one of the great names in the history of African exploration. He shares with Mungo Park the main honour of tracing the course of the River Niger, one of the central achievements of modern geographical discovery. Yet he is scarcely remembered as he deserves to be. He has, it is true, one substantial monument : a great granite column at the head of Lemon Street in Truro, erected in his honour shortly after his death. The column is a familiar sight to Cornishmen ; but few of them, I think, know much of the man it commemorates. Elsewhere in England he seems to be forgotten. Yet if ever a life could be called romantic, it was his. For this poor Cornish lad made four long journeys in Africa—at a time when one was more than enough for most people ; he described two of them in important books ; and he died at the age of twenty-nine.

He was born at Truro in 1804, a Cornishman on both sides of his family. His father kept a pub there—the Fighting Cocks, which later became the Dolphin. As it happened, he was born on the very day that Colonel Lemon was elected Member of Parliament for Truro : so his father (perhaps with an eye to his customers) gave the boy the second name of " Lemon "—Richard Lemon Lander.

There is nothing much to say about his early childhood.

He went to school in Truro and was a favourite with his master; but he said himself that he was always playing truant as a boy and that his chief delight was to hear tales of distant parts of the world. He was no more than nine when he left home; and at the ripe age of eleven he entered the service of a West India merchant and accompanied him across the Atlantic. After three years in the West Indies he came back to England and held for a time a succession of places as a gentleman's servant. Then in 1823 he took service with Major Colebrooke, who was being sent out by government on a mission of inquiry to the Cape of Good Hope. This gave Lander his first sight of Africa, the continent that had always excited his imagination most ardently : " there was a charm in the very sound of Africa ", he wrote later on, " that always made my heart flutter on hearing it mentioned ".[1] (It has been the same with many of the great African travellers, by the way, though they have not always put it quite like that. And once they have been there, no matter what sufferings they have undergone, they seem never to be fully happy anywhere else : Africa calls them back again and again, and many of the great ones have died there—Park and Livingstone and Baikie and Thomson.)

Lander travelled widely in South Africa with Colebrooke and then came home in 1824. He went back into service in England for a time; but he soon saw a chance of returning to Africa, and he seized it with both hands. In the summer of 1825 Captain Hugh Clapperton arrived home after making a long and important journey through North Africa with two English companions, and he was at once asked by the Colonial Secretary to go out again. The object of his second mission was primarily to open up trade relations with Sultan Bello of Sokoto, the most

[1] R. Lander, *Records of Captain Clapperton's Last Expedition* (1830), i. 11.

powerful state in what is now Northern Nigeria. But at
the same time Clapperton was also directed to try and
determine the course of the River Niger, which was then
a complete mystery. Mungo Park had explored the middle
section of the river ; but its source had not yet been found,
and—much more important—no one knew where it came
out into the sea. Some geographers indeed held that it
merely fell into a huge Central African lake : others that
Park's Niger was really the upper Nile. The true solution
to the problem was hardly guessed at.

As soon as he heard that Clapperton was going out to
Africa again, Richard Lander applied to go with him as
his servant. Clapperton agreed to take him on, and they
set out at the end of August. Three other Englishmen
were to accompany them, but they all died soon after
they arrived in Africa : so Clapperton and Lander were
without white companions for almost the whole of their
journey. Their plan was to approach Sokoto from the
south, starting from Badagri, a little to the west of Lagos
on the coast, making their way up to Bussa on the Niger
(the place where Mungo Park died) and crossing the river
there. They managed all this without difficulty, though
both of them were frequently ill on the way. From Bussa
they struck out north-east to Kano, the great commercial
centre of the whole of that region. Here Clapperton
decided to leave Lander behind with the heavy baggage,
going on to Sokoto by himself. When he had done his
business there, it was his intention to return and then to
proceed with Lander through the neighbouring kingdom
of Bornu and across the Sahara to Tripoli. But his plans
were upset by a war that was raging between Sokoto and
Bornu. He was delayed in endless negotiations with the
Sultan and finally had to send for Lander to join him.
When Lander arrived at Sokoto, the Sultan seized the

goods he brought, and the two of them were virtually prisoners.

In the account of the expedition that he subsequently wrote, Lander gives a touching description of their intense boredom and isolation at Sokoto, and the simple things they did to try and relieve it. " Before retiring to rest of an evening," he wrote, " cigars we had brought from England with us were generally produced ; and we inhaled their grateful fragrance oftentimes for an hour or two. This was the only luxury left us ; our tea and sugar had been consumed long before, and we fared in every respect like the Falatahs themselves. Squatted on mats in our huts, we spent the lingering hours in reading aloud, or chatting of our respective homes, and reciting village anecdotes . . . Sometimes, although neither of us was gifted with a voice of much power or compass, we attempted to sing a few English or Scotch tunes ; and sometimes I played others on my bugle-horn. How often have the pleasing strains of ' Sweet, sweet home ' resounded through the melancholy streets of Soccatoo! How often have its inhabitants listened with breathless attention to the music of the white-faced strangers, and observed to each other as they went away, ' Surely those Christians are sending a blessing to their country and friends ! ' "[1]

Clapperton was deeply indignant at the Sultan's behaviour. His plans were frustrated at every turn : he had been ill many times since his arrival in Africa, and his failure seems now to have preyed on his mind. In March 1827 he had a grave attack of dysentery, and it was soon plain that he was dying. He lingered on for a month, instructing Lander what he should do when he was left by himself, and he died on 13 April. Lander's account of

[1] ibid., ii. 60-1.

Clapperton's last illness is memorable and moving.[1]  He
was deeply attached to his master—after all, they had been
constant companions, in close intimacy, for eighteen
months—and he was grieved beyond measure at his death.
It left him, too, in a difficult, not to say dangerous, situation.
Here he was, at twenty-three, alone in a hostile country,
thousands of miles in any direction from white men's
assistance, charged with the duty of conveying Clapperton's
baggage and papers back to England.

He carried out his task with great skill and resource.
But it is characteristic of him that he did not content himself with following out his master's instructions to take
the easiest route home, by way of Tripoli.  His mind was
possessed by the problem of the Niger, and he determined
to try and solve it now.  He therefore started to make his
way back from Sokoto to the river, meaning then to
follow it down to the sea ; but he was balked by a hostile
local ruler and had to return to England by way of Badagri,
as he had come out.  He got home in the spring of 1828.

As soon as he had handed over his master's papers and
written up his account of the expedition, he begged the
Colonial Secretary to send him out again to make another
effort at determining the course of the Niger.  It is a
remarkable thing that he should have prevailed, for he
was very young and he had been nothing but Clapperton's
servant.  But the government decided to back him nevertheless, to equip him for his journey, to pay his wife a
modest annuity while he was away and a gratuity of £100
to himself when he should come back.  He was also allowed
to take with him his younger brother John as a companion,
unpaid.  They started at the beginning of 1830 and made
their way to Bussa, as before.  Thence it was their simple
plan to sail down the river until they reached the open

[1] ibid., ii. 63-76.

sea. That plan they exactly carried out, with remarkable speed. Within nine months of their arrival in Africa, the course of the Niger was a mystery no longer: the Landers had proved that it flowed through a great delta into the Bight of Benin.

Though their great journey was made so quickly, that does not mean that the Landers encountered no difficulties. On the contrary, they were more than once threatened with attack by people living on the banks of the river; and once they were actually set upon. They came through without disaster, chiefly through the imperturbable good sense of the two brothers, who refused to be provoked into avenging petty insults and threats. The virtues they showed are those of nearly all the greatest African travellers: resourcefulness, courage, humanity—above all, a never-failing patience. It was that combination of qualities that carried them through.

They had made a discovery of the highest importance. The problem had been much in the minds of Englishmen for forty years past and had perplexed geographers ever since the time of Herodotus. They were warmly welcomed when they arrived home. Richard received an outstanding honour: he was the very first traveller to be awarded the gold medal of the Royal Geographical Society, which was founded in 1831. And the brothers got some things, too, of more solid value than a welcome: a thousand guineas, for instance, from John Murray for the book in which they described their achievement. It appeared in 1832 as the *Journal of an Expedition to explore the Course and Termination of the Niger*: three pretty little volumes published at 5s. each in the celebrated " Family Library ". The book is delightfully readable still—the story of a great feat of exploration told in a style of *naïve* and engaging charm.

It was natural that their discovery should now be

exploited for its commercial value : natural too that the traders who were interested should invite Richard Lander to go back to Africa once more, to pilot and assist their work. He consented. An expedition was quickly fitted up (including an iron steamer, the *Quorra*, that was to be tried out on the Niger), and it sailed in the summer of 1832. The venture was unlucky from the start : there were personal disagreements among the leaders and the sailors, the equipment was defective and inadequate. But Richard Lander comes out of the story with undamaged credit, an admirable colleague and guide. It was a stroke of cruel luck that he should have been involved in a skirmish with the people of a small place called Angiama in the delta. The circumstances are not entirely clear. It seems that at some village in the Nun mouth of the Niger Lander's men were twice attacked when they went on shore to get wood. The *Quorra* then fired her gun at intervals as a warning to the people, and as they continued to show their hostility the crew landed and the place was burnt. That at least was the story told in a letter written at the time, which appears to be well informed.[1] If it is true, this is the only occasion on which Lander departed from the policy of strict forbearance in the face of provoca-tion, which he had steadfastly followed in all his earlier journeys. Some weeks later, sailing up the Brass River, he ran into an ambush. " So great was Lander's confidence in the sincerity and good will of the natives that he could not at first believe that the destructive fire, by which he was literally surrounded, was anything more than a mode of salutation they had adopted in honour of his arrival."[2] When he was convinced of his mistake he led the defence of his men with energy. But he was seriously wounded

---

[1] R. Huish, *The Travels of Richard Lander* (1836), 762.
[2] ibid., 771.

and compelled to retreat downstream in a small canoe. Together with the survivors of the party he made his way across to Fernando Po, where he arrived on 25 January 1834. His wound proved fatal and he died on 2 February.

Richard Lander was a little man, but broad-shouldered and very strong. His character is easily made out from his life, his writings, and what other people said about him. He was affectionate, gentle, gay ; his mind was quick and sensible ; his courage, his sweet temper were unfailing. He deserves to be remembered rather more faithfully, perhaps, than he has been in the past. And so, if you are ever in Truro, look up at that granite column, and think for a moment of Richard Lander—the merry, heroic, young Cornishman who solved the great riddle of the Niger.

# THE VICTORIAN PROCONSULS

In the course of Queen Victoria's reign the British Empire
expanded with an astonishing rapidity : in North America,
in Africa, in India and the Far East and Australasia—
everywhere it was the same. But what strikes one most
about this Victorian expansion is not really its speed : it
is the haphazard, almost casual way in which so much of
it came about. In a familiar phrase, much misunderstood,
Seeley said that England seemed, " as it were, to have
conquered and peopled half the world in a fit of absence
of mind ". He meant, of course, that the great majority
of Englishmen thought little about the Empire: as he went
on to add, " we constantly betray by our modes of speech
that we do not reckon our colonies as really belonging to
us ". That was true when he wrote, in 1883 ; and for all
the efforts of conscious imperialists like himself, it has
remained true ever since. The interest of Englishmen in
the Empire has always been vague and intermittent.

But that does not mean that there were no fixed
principles on which British imperial policy was based,
that Downing Street and the proconsuls merely devised
solutions to the problems that confronted them as they
turned up one by one. On the contrary, Victorian colonial
policy bears a strongly-marked character of its own. It
inherited great principles from the past, dropped some of
them, modified others, contributed much that was new ;

and handed on a powerful tradition that profoundly
influences—it often dominates—our colonial policy today.

The first and greatest thing that the Victorians took
over from the eighteenth century was the humanitarian
tradition, which attained the highest point of its influence
in the emancipation of the slaves, four years before Victoria
came to the throne. It is interesting to see how that tradition
fared as the century went on. In the West Indies the
working of the Emancipation Act was far from an un-
qualified success. The officials on the spot pointed constantly to its defects, and especially to the inadequate
provision it made for the difficult transition from slavery
to freedom. Here is the Governor of Trinidad, writing in
1848 : " One of the many errors which have been committed since the granting of emancipation is the little
attention paid to any legislation having for its end the
formation of a society on true, sound and lasting principles.
. . . As the question at present stands, a race has been freed,
but a society has not been formed."[1]

For already in the forties a reaction against the older
humanitarianism had set in. The movement had done a
good deal to discredit itself. The Niger expedition of 1841
was a disastrous, a disgraceful failure ; and Dickens voiced,
as usual, much of the feeling of his class when he attacked
its promoters, the whole plan upon which it had been
based, what he called " the ocean of ignorance at Exeter
Hall ".[2] The humanitarians had had their triumphs, but
they had been with limited, fixed objectives. The prohibition of the slave trade, the freeing of the slaves—these
were clear ends in themselves ; when it came to more
complex problems, demanding a close knowledge of West

---

[1] K. N. Bell and W. P. Morrell (ed.), *Select Documents on British Colonial Policy*
1830-1860 (1928), 432.
[2] Charles Dickens, *Miscellaneous Papers* (1914), 123.

Indian or African or Maori society, a new approach was needed.

It came in the fifties, and most of all from Livingstone. He knew what he was talking about, as none of his predecessors had done ; for he had lived and worked in Africa for fifteen years before he first spoke out. To him that union of " Christianity and commerce " which had been advocated so incompetently by the promoters of the Niger expedition remained the right policy—the only policy to exterminate the Arab slave trade that was ravaging Central Africa when he saw it. But he understood that no quick triumph could be expected, that the old African order was breaking down, that it must be replaced with something else, which would be the work of many years of experiment. For that, the first thing necessary was a clearer understanding of the African, and it was to this that Livingstone addressed himself. He had an instinctive sympathy with Africans (a much closer sympathy than with his own countrymen), he had infinite patience with them, and something rarer, especially among missionaries : a real detachment, a disinterested mind. His passion was for the truth at any cost, even if it went against his own preconceptions, against Christianity itself. So you find him, quite early in his career, stating the case of the tribal rain-doctor, and later on inquiring pertinaciously of his brother-in-law—a missionary of a more orthodox kind—what was the real nature of initiation rites.[1]

Livingstone went, in fact, some way towards the approach of the modern sociologist. He stands at the turning-point between the old humanitarianism and the new. In the second half of the century, as the Victorians were faced with a constantly-increasing responsibility for

[1] D. Livingstone, *Missionary Travels and Researches in South Africa* (1857), 22-5 ; *The Matabele Mission*, ed. J. P. R. Wallis (1945), 11.

P.E.                                                                    O

the government of primitive peoples, they developed a fresh
technique : what has come in the twentieth century to be
called " indirect rule ". Its fundamental principle—that
of ruling a dependent people as far as possible through
their traditional institutions—was not novel. But the later
Victorians turned something that had been merely a convenient device of administration into a system of government designed for the positive benefit of the people themselves : it was a new application of the principle of
" trusteeship " they had inherited from Burke. And that
system has played a vital part in our colonial policy in the
twentieth century—nor in ours alone, for it has influenced
French and Belgian practice too.

The principles of indirect rule were tried out and
formulated in the colonies themselves, in Africa and
Malaya and the Pacific. They were not in any sense the
work of London, the Colonial Office, which wisely left
such matters to the decision of the men on the spot. The
makers of indirect rule were men like Sir Arthur Gordon
in Fiji in the seventies and above all, at the end of the
century, Sir George Goldie and Frederick Lugard in
Africa : Goldie, the founder of the United Africa Company
and its all-powerful director, who laid down with accuracy
and imagination the lines on which the administration of
Nigeria should develop ; Lugard, the young army officer
who went out to tropical Africa, almost by chance, in the
nineties and stayed to make his life's work there. As
Lugard wrote of Uganda in 1893 : " An arbitrary and
despotic rule, which takes no account of native customs,
traditions, and prejudices, is not suited to the successful
development of an infant civilisation, nor, in my view, is
it in accordance with the spirit of British colonial rule.
The king has been proved incompetent and useless, but

the Resident should rule through and by the chiefs."[1]
Here was a new conception of colonial government : it
has proved very fruitful in our own time, and we owe it
entirely to the Victorians.

It would be a mistake, however, to suppose that the
Victorian Empire was run solely by men with such robust
and positive ideas. The early Victorians had been very
doubtful whether the Empire would, or should, survive
at all. In the forties and fifties responsible government was
conceded to the colonies of white settlement in North
America, Australia, and New Zealand ; and very few
people believed firmly in the permanence of their imperial
connexion with England. Sir James Stephen, the powerful
head of the Colonial Office, wrote in a gloomy mood in
1846 : " There are, at this moment, in Canada almost as
many Europeans as there were in the United States when
they declared their independence—a very pregnant fact in
many ways."[2]

There was similar doubt over the future of the dependent
colonies. To many Englishmen they seemed valueless :
the West Indies, a group of islands whose prosperity had
gone for ever, sinking into visible, rapid decay ; the West
African settlements, a series of posts in a pestilential and
disappointing country. In the sixties the House of Commons
showed itself anxious to undertake no further commitments
there. A senior member of the Colonial Office summed
up the problems of its government with remarkable
honesty and clearness, minuting on a despatch from Lagos
in 1862 : " How long ought a man to take before he
believes himself a good judge of the relative merits of
obscure African tribes and villages ? . . . We want to use
the different tribes as a means of extinguishing slave-dealing

[1] Quoted in J. Simmons (ed.), *From Empire to Commonwealth* (1949), 178.
[2] ibid., 134.

amongst themselves and those around them, whilst they want to use us as a means of oppressing their neighbours, and there seems to me to be a constant trial going on which shall be the tool of the other. . . . Wherever we go in Africa, our views are as enlightened and lofty, compared with those of the barbarous people amongst whom we find ourselves, as those of a superior race of beings : and if we choose to employ steamers and a few disciplined troops, our influence is paramount. The apparent good is so great that it is very fascinating. But still one cannot help occasionally asking oneself, where is it to end ? It is also uncomfortable to reflect on the disparity between our power and our knowledge. The first is so tremendous that we can at will exalt or destroy, but who is to ensure us a corresponding discrimination ? I feel afraid sometimes lest we should be like the kings in burlesques who with comical vigour despatch one slave with a blow and cover the other with honours, long before they can know whether either deserves his fate.[1]" In plain matter-of-fact civil servant's prose, this is something very near to the mood of " Dover Beach ". How easy it is to over-estimate the complacency of the Victorians !

It was not often, indeed, that doubts so grave were expressed with so much frankness. And gradually, in the eighties and nineties, a new spirit, tougher and more self-confident, appeared in British colonial administration. A new efficiency too, for here as in other branches of the Civil Service the reforms of the fifties and sixties had had their effect. The old system was based on a few simple rules, applied with an infinite talent for improvisation. Towards the end of the century the rules became rapidly more numerous, the scope of the individual less and less. In the Colonial Office, that is ; for in the colonies them-

[1] ibid., 158-9.

selves the officials retained a real measure of initiative and independence a good deal longer than their colleagues in London.

We often speak of the closing years of the Queen's reign as a time of extravagant imperialism. But that jingoism, raucous and strident, was not as important as it is often made to appear. It was not characteristic of England, and its effects were transient. The nineties have much more positive and permanent achievements to show, in the development of the tropical African protectorates and the administrative reforms of Joseph Chamberlain. Chamberlain's work as Secretary of State for the Colonies has hardly received the full recognition it deserves. So much of his eight years at the Colonial Office was passed in the glare of furious public controversy that a great deal of his quieter and more solid achievement has remained unnoticed. But his Secretaryship does mark an important new stage in the history of the dependent Empire. It was he who first proclaimed an imaginative programme for the planned economic development of the colonies—a policy modestly begun in his own time, but leading directly to the Colonial Development Acts that have been passed since 1929.

His work for the Colonial Civil Service was no less important. To take only one instance : he was the driving force behind the application of the new methods of preventive medicine in West Africa, the outward sign of which was the creation of the West African Medical Staff as a unified service in 1902. Mary Kingsley—who fought Chamberlain more than once, and fiercely, on other issues —paid him a ringing tribute. It was in her last lecture, delivered in London in February 1900. (She sailed off next month to become a nurse in the Boer War, caught enteric, and died at Simonstown early in June.) " Mr.

Chamberlain in this matter has done a grand good thing,"
she said, " and done it nobly, for no one urged it on him,
it was done to catch no votes—white men in West Africa
have none. It was not done to add to his own reputation
or glorification as a statesman ; he has given time, thought
and labour to it that he could, had he cared for that end,
have spent in advertising himself. It was done from
humane sympathy alone."[1]  Looking back over the career
of that formidable Birmingham man, so masterful, in many
things so uncongenial, the hard lines of his character soften
for a moment, he becomes alive, something more than a
mere efficient Cabinet Minister : one begins to understand
why it was that so many of his subordinates held him in
a respect that was tinged with affection.

Over against Chamberlain, his unwearied and venomous
opponents, stand the anti-imperialists—an oddly-assorted
group of Little Englanders, Liberals and Labour men. They
too have positive achievements to show : in Hobson's
book *Imperialism*, which influenced the mind of Lenin so
much ; and in the pro-Boers' passionate, and bitterly
unpopular, denunciation of the South African war. There
was in that much exaggeration, wrong-headedness and
spite : yet when the war was over and the time for a
settlement came, the Dutch South Africans remembered
and trusted the Englishmen who had championed them,
as they could never have trusted Milner and the Con-
servatives.

The pro-Boers based themselves on a simple appeal to
justice. Here they took strong ground. For justice was
the declared objective of Victorian colonial policy—above
all, justice between races, the most difficult sort to ensure ;
between British and French Canadians, between Africans
and Dutch and British at the Cape, between settlers and

[1] Mary Kingsley, *West African Studies* (ed. 2, 1901), 439.

Maoris in New Zealand. The problem arose in many different forms in India. Macaulay had been faced with it in 1836 over the " Black Act ", which established an entirely equal system of justice for Indians and Englishmen in Bengal : he maintained his position firmly and so earned the malignant hatred of some sections of British society in Calcutta.[1] Elgin, as Viceroy of India at the end of his life, met the same problem in another form, when he was strongly pressed to reprieve an English soldier who had murdered an Indian. He was inflexible. " The verdict was clearly borne out by the evidence ", so he told the Secretary of State. " The sentence was in accordance with the law, and the judge, to whom I referred, saw no reason to question it. The decision of the Governor-General in Council was that the law must take its course."[2]

This steady, even justice was something that could be administered only by a paternal government, acting as arbiter between races, creeds and classes, where their interests were in conflict. And indeed Victorian imperialism remained paternal in its ideals to the end. Here was something on which all the great proconsuls were at one, whatever their other differences. Cromer's view is characteristic : " Our primary duty is not to introduce a system which, under the specious cloak of free institutions, will enable a small minority of natives to misgovern their countrymen, but to establish one which will enable the mass of the population to be governed according to the code of Christian morality."[3]

The Victorians lacked sympathy with the intellectuals, the educated minority, whether in Egypt or in India—though it is fair to remember that it was an Englishman, a retired Civil Servant, who did most towards founding the

[1] See *Lord Macaulay's Legislative Minutes*, ed. C. D. Dharker (1946), 47-58, 168-97.
[2] Quoted in Simmons, *From Empire to Commonwealth*, 160-1.
[3] ibid., 201.

Indian National Congress ; and that though Lord Dufferin, the Viceroy, forbade the association of officials with it, he approved of the Congress in principle at its outset. For " the mass of the population ", on the other hand, the Victorians did a magnificent work, with affection and boundless energy : ending slave-raids in Nigeria and civil wars in Malaya, establishing security and peace and justice when those things had been forgotten or never known before. So much of it is summed up in that single story of Kipling's, " William the Conqueror " ; for when all has been said about constitutions and laws, the Indian Famine Code may stand for the greatest work of the Victorian proconsuls.

# THE BRITISH IMPERIAL TRADITION

SINCE THE end of the Second World War a transformation has come over the British Commonwealth. Until 1947 there were five Dominions, all of them peopled, or at least controlled, by Europeans : three more have now been added, all of them wholly Asiatic in population. This increase has been balanced by the secession of Eire, her decision, after long havering, to set up as an entirely independent state. Burma, too, has chosen independence outside the Commonwealth rather than the Dominion Status she was offered within it. As for what we have been accustomed to call the Dependent Empire—that phrase is quickly becoming obsolete. Everywhere—in the West Indies, in Africa, in South-East Asia—the colonies seem to be racing ahead towards self-government, though, even so, they are not moving as fast as some of their own people would like.

But it is not only a political transformation that we are seeing. There has been a change in the field of economics that has been of almost equal importance. Since 1945, when the second Colonial Development and Welfare Act was passed, Britain has begun to pour money into her colonies at a speed and on a scale that have never hitherto been approached. The great African groundnuts project was a spectacular, and a controversial, example : but it was only one project among a hundred, large and small.

We cannot claim, in our generation, to have invented the principle of colonial self-government; and the idea of a deliberate, planned investment of public money in the colonies can be traced directly to Joseph Chamberlain, and indeed much further back into the nineteenth century. What is new today is the speed with which both these principles are being applied.

To many people it is a matter for grave misgiving. They agree without question, as we all do, that the old Dominions, the colonies of white settlement, should enjoy full independence within the Commonwealth; but they question the wisdom of extending that principle to Africans and Asiatics—people with very different political traditions from those of western Europe, with a shorter experience, or almost none, of the responsibilities of self-government. In effect, they say, it does not mean an extension of democracy: it means handing over an ignorant majority to the control of a clique of grasping and incapable politicians. It is hypocritical, in their view, to argue that there is wisdom or justice in this policy. It is a policy of " scuttle "—to quote a die-hard's phrase; of running away from our responsibilities; of a craven panic, brought on by the weakening of Britain's power in world politics.

It is not the first time that cries of this kind have been heard in England. Just over a hundred years ago, in 1837, there were two small rebellions in Canada. They were trifling in themselves, mopped up in a few days; but they were a danger-signal that could not be mistaken, a warning that the persistent demand of the Canadians for some control over their own affairs was not to be ignored. As a result, Lord Durham was dispatched on his great mission to inquire into the whole story and to recommend what should be done to remedy the Canadians' grievances. In his Report he advised that most of their demands—all those that were really important—should be met; that self-government should be conceded to them, frankly and immediately, in almost the whole of their domestic affairs. When that Report was published, it was received with a storm of abuse by British and Canadian Tories. If Durham's proposals were adopted, they swore it would mean the end of the British Empire. Give the Canadians an inch, they said, and they'll take an ell: in a few years' time they will have left the Empire altogether, to set up on their own or to join the United States.

These criticisms were not without their effect upon Lord Melbourne's government. It refused to accept Durham's recommendations to their full extent, preferring to proceed timidly, though still in the same direction; and it was another twenty years before self-government was firmly established in Canada. The die-hards went on prophesying disaster, taunting successive British governments with yielding to Canadian pressure instead of standing firm. But they were proved wrong. Self-governing Canada did not become independent Canada: neither was it absorbed in the United States. Instead, in 1867 all the British colonies in North America, except Newfoundland, came together to form a single federation, which has remained steadfastly loyal to the British connexion ever since. In the first World War Canada raised a force of 650,000 men; in the second, one of more than a million.

Time after time in these last few years, as I have watched the great changes coming over the Commonwealth, my mind has gone back into the history of its development in the past, to situations like that I have just mentioned, which bear some resemblance to our own. Sometimes I have found that this reflection fortified me, in a spell of

depression, sometimes it seemed to offer a warning : either
way, it has usually instructed me. To this thinking about
the past I have added some discussion with friends who
have actually been confronting the problems of our imperial
government in the last few years—on the North-West
Frontier of India, in Nigeria, in Malaya. As a result, I
have become deeply interested in one question above all—
or rather, I should say, a group of questions. What are
the fundamental principles of British imperial government ?
What is there that is distinctive about them, found with
us and not in the other empires of the world ? Where do
these principles spring from—if they exist at all ? In other
words, is there a British imperial tradition ?

The British Empire was founded first of all upon trade.
That is nothing unique—the same is true of all the other
great modern empires of the world. But it is, I think, fair
to say that trade has taken a relatively greater share in the
development of the British Empire than in that of its
counterparts. It was trade, first and foremost, that took
Englishmen to the West Indies, to Africa, to India and
Malaya and the Far East. This is a fact, not open to dispute, and it is in my view very foolish for Englishmen to
feel in any way ashamed of it. The British Empire, and
imperialism of all kinds, have been so constantly under
attack in the last half-century that we have many of us
acquired a sort of guilty conscience, particularly on this
point, as if the trade had been dishonestly come by and
conducted against the interests of the rest of the world.
Looking at this trade as a whole—at the means by which
it was founded and sustained, at the results it has led to,
not for Britain only but for other countries too—I can see
no justification whatever for regretting it. There were
black spots in this trade, of which I shall have something

more to say in a moment.  But I am speaking now of our imperial commerce as a whole, and considering it in that light I cannot but think its development has brought great material benefit to the whole world.

It is perhaps characteristic of us as a people that we have been forgetful of the memory of the men who built up this trade.  The capitalists, the bankers and merchants, in the first place : they are few of them remembered now, except when by accident some grateful and demonstrative contemporary saw fit to commemorate them.  Here is Sir Thomas Smith, for instance, who amassed one of the great Elizabethan fortunes, much of which he invested in the ventures of the East India and Muscovy Companies. It is ironical to find that his name is perpetuated, not in India or at Archangel, but in Smith's Sound off the coast of Greenland.  It was so christened by William Baffin, the leader of one of that long series of expeditions to discover the North-West Passage.  Like its fellows, that voyage came to nothing ; but Baffin felt gratitude to the great London capitalist who had backed him, and he paid him the one small tribute in his power—a tribute that still stands after three centuries and a half.

But such tributes are rare.  We honour the names— justly or inadequately—of the politicians, the administrators, the explorers and soldiers and sailors, who built up the empire ; but we seldom think of the capitalists who did so much to make their work possible.  I suppose we may say, " They have their reward " : but that is no more than a niggardly, feeble excuse.  They made their profits —and some of them were very handsome : yes, but we are apt to forget their losses, the courage and daring and imagination, the hard brain-work, that lay behind the projects they fathered and backed.  Of the whole race, I suppose Cecil Rhodes is the only one who is generally

remembered : the least characteristic of them, a man of a
lonely and curious genius, attractive at once and repellent.
He stands quite apart from his fellows, one of the strangest
men in our history.  No : the sort of capitalist I am thinking
of is Macgregor Laird, the Birkenhead shipbuilder, who
spent two years on the Niger himself and then another
twenty at home, persistently working for the development
of British trade on the river.  It was all in the way of
business.  But then so is a politician's work, or an actor's ;
and we do not forget Burleigh or Garrick because in the
course of their careers they made handsome fortunes.

But if we are unjust to the memory of these great
capitalists and merchants, I think we have been more
ungrateful still to the small fry, the practical men, the
seamen and traders upon whom the day-to-day business
of building up the British commercial empire fell.  They
too may have done well enough and retired in late middle
age to their snug little houses at Lyme Regis or Topsham
or Falmouth : but those were the lucky ones, and they
worked hard enough, and ran through great dangers, to
achieve that modest measure of comfort.  Far more of
them died younger, in the cold Canadian North or in those
pestilent swamps where so much of their work lay—in
Malaya, in the evil deltas of the Hooghly and the Niger.
Or they died at sea.  Here is a young fellow named Ching,
modestly commemorated in the parish church of Launceston
in Cornwall, " who in the month of August 1834 "—he
was twenty-two—" after having been wrecked in the ship
*Charles Eaton* on a voyage to China suffered a more cruel
fate at the hands of ignorant savages, by whom the crew
were decoyed and murdered in the island of Boydang in
Torres Straits ".

They were a tough, hard-headed lot, these men.  The

bargains they drove were stiff, their practice sometimes very sharp. Yet continued sharp practice cannot be the foundation of a prosperous and lasting trade. If they had not been, taken all round, a decent race of men who stuck to their word, they would never have built up as they did, fragment by fragment, the great reef of British imperial trade in all the quarters of the world.

They have found only two champions, only two people with the imaginative perception to discern the great work they were doing. One of those two was a foreigner, Joseph Conrad; the other a woman, Mary Kingsley. Mary Kingsley's affection for the " coaster ", the gruff, uncouth British trader in West Africa, was unsentimental. " The trader ", she says, " is practically dealing single-handed with the native authorities, and is regarded by them in much the same light as they regard one of their great spirits—as an undoubtedly superior, different sort of creation from themselves, yet as one who is likewise interested in mundane affairs, and whom they try to manage and propitiate and bully for their own advantage ; while the trader, on his part, gets to know them so well during this process that he usually gets fond of them, as all white men who really know Africans always do, and looks after them when they are sick, or in trouble, and tries to keep them at peace with each other and with the white government, for on peace depends the prosperity that means trade. Therefore on the whole the trader knows his African better than all the other sorts of white men put together."[1]

That is a portrait of a type. The individual is still harder to recover. These men were not communicative, and they rarely had articulate friends. Perhaps, beside that portrait of the ordinary West African trader, we may put

[1] S. Gwynn, *The Life of Mary Kingsley* (ed. 2, 1933), 48.

that of a less ordinary captain in the East India Company's service, to remind us of the great range of men who are to be found in the class I am considering. I am thinking of John Wordsworth, who went down off Weymouth with his ship the *Earl of Abergavenny* on the voyage to India in 1805. His loss was the cruellest blow that his brother William ever suffered. It drew from him a series of letters and poems in which he described John's character and mind. From them a picture emerges, singularly pure and noble : shy, self-contained, grave (" his mess-mates used to call him the Philosopher "), generous, unselfish, and, in a famous phrase, " a poet in everything but words ". As William wrote, heartbroken, on the night that the news reached him, " John was very dear to me and my heart will never forget him ".[1]

Not many English sea-captains, perhaps, were like that. And by contrast there is, of course, a different side to the story. This trade brought England prosperity, material comfort—sugar and soap and rubber and tea and tin : it made possible a higher standard of living for every one, poor and rich. But it also brought war, above all in the eighteenth century, when we fought the French and the Spaniards repeatedly for colonies and trade. It would be childish to deny that it was these trade disputes that led us into war—most clearly in 1739, when Britain was dragged into fighting Spain in the interests of a powerful commercial company and against the earnest wish of both the British and the Spanish governments. And yet we must also remember that in the nineteenth century, by contrast, trade brought peace. British naval supremacy was then unquestioned, and it was used for the preservation of peace as an essential condition for the limit-

[1] Fenwick note to " The Character of the Happy Warrior " : *Poetical Works* (ed. De Selincourt and Darbishire), iv. 419 ; *The Early Letters of William and Dorothy Wordsworth* (1935), 446-7.

less development of British trade in every part of the world. For the British Empire was not only, as I have said, a trading empire, to a peculiar degree: in the nineteenth and twentieth centuries it became a free-trading empire.

Here is a strong contrast to almost all its neighbours and rivals. The French, the Dutch, the Portuguese, kept their empires closed, as far as they could—for French, for Dutch, for Portuguese traders only. They never achieved entire self-sufficiency, any more than Hitler's Germany in the 1930s : but the greatest measure of self-sufficiency was their avowed objective. Britain worked on different lines. The long lead she had established in industrial development, and her own dependence upon cheap and plentiful imports of raw materials, made free trade a vital interest to her. And what was really a vital interest became in the course of time—it was the way of the Victorians—something like a religious dogma. One striking, almost comic, example may be given. In 1859 the Canadian government imposed a tariff that was directed against imports from Britain as well as from foreign countries. The manufacturers of Sheffield attempted to persuade the Secretary of State for the Colonies to disallow the tariff. In the course of the memorial they submitted in support of their case they asked " that the policy of protection to native manufacturers in Canada should be distinctly discountenanced by Her Majesty's Government, as a system condemned by reason and experience, directly contrary to the policy solemnly adopted by the Mother Country, and calculated to breed disunion and distrust between Great Britain and her colonies. It cannot be regarded as less than indecent, and a reproach, that, while for fifteen years the government, the greatest statesmen, and the press of this country have been not only advocating but practising the principles of free trade, the government of one of her most important colonies should have been advocating monopoly and protection."[1]

The facts of the matter are clear enough. Free trade was a British interest. But it was also a principle that helped other people and made for the peace of the world. It is hypocritical to suggest that Britain adopted the policy for moral reasons : the reasons were plainly commercial. But it is merely stupid to deny that the policy also benefited others at the same time. (After all, the same thing is to be seen, over and over again, in European politics. Time after time Britain becomes the mainspring behind a coalition of powers threatened by the domination of one : Spain in the sixteenth century, France in the seventeenth and eighteenth, Germany in the twentieth. Again it is not because of any superior virtue in Britain, but because it is in her interest : yet that interest coincides with the interests of others.)

So you find the British Empire, for example, standing over against the Dutch in the East Indies and South-East Asia in the early nineteenth century. British traders repeatedly asserted that the Dutch were doing their best to shut them out : the Dutch as frequently replied with the blandest contradictions of their complaints. It was Stamford Raffles who provided the answer in founding Singapore, with the declared purpose of making it at once the focus of trade between the Indian Ocean and the China Seas and one of the great free ports of the world : free to all comers —British, Dutch, Malay, Chinese, American alike. His judgment was sure. Within fifty years of its foundation it was a port with trade worth more than £13 million a

---

[1] A. B. Keith (ed.), *Selected Speeches and Documents on British Colonial Policy* (1918), ii. 55-6.

year : in 1939 it was reckoned one of the ten greatest ports of the world.

I have been speaking so far of what may at all times be called " legitimate " trade—trade, that is, that did nobody any harm if it was honestly and peaceably conducted. But there were other trades too, of another character ; and one above all, the slave trade. It seems to be a common illusion that Britain began the slave trade—began it in the 1560s with the voyages of Sir John Hawkins to West Africa. An interesting illustration, that, of our national habit of super-fluous repentance, of what psychologists might describe as the operation of a guilt-complex. For of course it is a complete error. The slave trade was already highly developed at that time, the Spanish government contract-ing, usually with Portuguese and Germans and other foreigners, for the regular supply of slaves to work in their American colonies. It was not for another hundred years that Englishmen began to take a really large share in the trade. But once they had entered seriously upon it, they took it up with energy. In the course of the eighteenth century Britain became by far the biggest participator in the trade, and Liverpool its greatest headquarters in Europe.

The Atlantic slave trade is a most important subject that cries out for a first-class economic historian. As things are, until somebody has sifted the mass of statistics that are available—unreliable as they often are, conflicting and incomplete—we cannot give a good answer to any of the most obvious questions that arise. How many slaves were transported ? How many of them died on the way ? What prices did they fetch in Africa, and in the New World when they were sold to the planters ? What net profit did the traders make ? And what was the real importance of the trade to the ports upon which it was based, to Liverpool and Bristol and Nantes ?

Those are all questions that we cannot yet answer satisfactorily. All we can say with truth is that the trade was a powerful and wealthy one and that in the eighteenth century the greatest share of its profits went to Englishmen. There is no need to enlarge on its cruelties, for every one now is agreed that it was a cruel and disgusting business. Its worst effects are not, I think, to be sought among the slaves who were actually transported. Their lives on the plantations of the New World were often dreadful enough : but worse still was the effect of the trade upon Africa, the source whence they all came. It is hardly possible to exaggerate the evil it did there : in shutting out all other trades, in wholesale depopulation, in promoting slave-raids and inter-tribal warfare. One need only recall Livingstone's sober, considered estimate, that for every slave who reached America, five had died in Africa.[1]

But if Englishmen thus took over the lead in carrying on the trade, they also directed its abolition. Britain was not in fact the first power to prohibit the trade to its subjects : Denmark did so in 1792. But the Danish slave trade was of unimportant magnitude. It was Britain's action in proscribing it in 1807 that really marked the decisive step towards its complete suppression. We all remember Wilberforce's name in this connexion—and quite rightly. But I think it is often supposed that from that time onwards the slave trade quickly died out all over the world, as if, in some magic way, when Britain prohibited the trade to her own subjects it withered everywhere of its own accord. That is very far from being true. It was another sixty years before all the great Western powers

[1] D. and C. Livingstone, *Narrative of an Expedition to the Zambesi and its Tributaries* (1865), 392.

agreed to prohibit the trade, and twenty more years before it was conquered in the Indian Ocean. Now the main instruments in killing it were the British Foreign Office, British diplomacy, the British navy. From 1814 onwards the prohibition of the trade formed a settled part of British foreign policy. It involved endless negotiation with foreign powers, with Portugal and Spain, above all with France and the United States. If you go to the archives of the Foreign Office you will find a vast file of correspondence—over a thousand volumes of it—bearing the one title " Slave Trade " : there lies the record of all the pertinacity, the patience, the single-minded energy that went into that thankless task. Thankless, and expensive : for it cost Britain thousands of lives and millions of pounds —impossible to estimate how many—spent in bribing other powers to give their consent to treaties for the effective suppression of the trade and in maintaining squadrons of the navy off the coasts of Africa to search for and capture the slave-ships.

And why ? What did Britain get in return for all this money that she spent ? Something material, indeed : for once she had made up her mind to prohibit the trade to her own subjects, it was clearly to her interest that it should be brought to an end everywhere. But this is not the full explanation, and any one who attempts to argue that it is must be completely ignorant of the temper of the British Parliament and people of that time. The truth is simple, and fundamental : that Englishmen, once roused to a knowledge of what the trade was really like, had made up their minds that it must be ended—everywhere, once and for all.

It is the classic example of the influence of the humanitarians on British colonial policy. But it is worth while to notice that that does not mean solely the influence of missionaries and religious bodies. It would be hard to find in the nineteenth century a more pagan character than Palmerston : noisy, cheerful, buoyed up on his own perpetual self-confidence, an old-fashioned aristocrat without a shred of natural piety in him. Yet it was Palmerston, among all English politicians, who did most for the prohibition of the foreign slave trade, working steadily to that end with all the force at his command up to the very close of his career. " During the many years that I was at the Foreign Office," he wrote as an old man, " there was no subject that more constantly or more intensely occupied my thoughts, or constituted the aim of my labours. . . . The achievement which I look back to with the greatest and purest pleasure was the forcing the Brazilians to give up their slave trade."[1]

Nor is that exceptional. The missionaries and the religious bodies had a great influence on British colonial policy. But it was not an influence exercised against the opposition of more worldly-minded civil servants and politicians : it was effective precisely because those two parties were on the whole in agreement. The humanitarian tradition became deeply implanted in the Colonial Office under Sir James Stephen—one of the unregarded great men of Early Victorian England, the most powerful and perhaps the ablest permanent head that the Office has known. Ever since then it has been at all times a discernible strand in British colonial policy : a genuine attempt has been made to conceive of colonial government as something that exists for the benefit of the people who are to be governed and not primarily for the convenience or profit of the governors.

Here again it would be wrong to suggest that this is

---

[1] H. W. V. Temperley and L. M. Penson (ed.), *Foundations of British Foreign Policy* (1938), 304.

a principle peculiar to Britain. There have been humanitarians elsewhere, figures equally majestic and lofty—Las
Casas in the Spanish empire, Lavigerie in the French. The
difference is once more a difference of degree, not of kind.
Humanitarian ideas have exercised a more powerful, a
more continuous, influence on our imperial policy than
on French or Spanish or Dutch : they have not been, as
it were, injected into it from time to time, they are part
of the very marrow of its bones.

This influence has been exercised in two ways. First,
from outside, through constant criticism of the Colonial
Office and its actions in Parliament and the press. It has
been one of the greatest services of the humanitarians to
keep colonial questions continually in the minds of Englishmen, to promote a watchful, well-informed, independent
examination of the doings of Secretaries of State and civil
servants. It is against the traditions of English law to
confer any special privileges upon our civil servants as
such, to exempt them from ordinary legal processes as the
French do, to some extent, under their *droit administratif*.
You can see this again and again : at its most striking,
perhaps, in the vehement attacks that have sometimes
been made upon civil servants and military officers who are
faced with grave crises, perhaps incipient rebellion, and
use force for its prompt suppression, as Lord Torrington
did in Ceylon in 1848, and Governor Eyre in Jamaica in
1865, and—coming down nearer to our own time—General
Dyer at Amritsar in 1919. Each of these men was faced
with the gravest of decisions : whether to use the troops at
his command for the immediate extinction of the trouble, or
to hold them in, allowing the disorder to spread, trying
still to end it by persuasion and moral force. Each of them
in the end decided to make full use of his troops, and each
believed sincerely that he had thereby prevented far worse

disorder, perhaps civil war. But each was fiercely attacked at home. Inquiries into their action were pressed for and secured; and when Eyre, for example, as a result of the inquiry was relieved of his post and came back to England he was twice prosecuted for the murder of one of the leaders of the Jamaican revolt, G. W. Gordon.

Now notice that this was done, not by some aggrieved crank, but under the direction of a " Jamaica Committee " formed specially for the purpose, with John Stuart Mill for its chairman and T. H. Huxley and Herbert Spencer among its members. Huxley's position is most instructive. It is set out, with all his habitual lucidity, in a letter he wrote to a newspaper at the time. " I do not presume to speak with authority on a legal question ", he wrote; " but, unless I am misinformed, English law does not permit good persons, as such, to strangle bad persons, as such. On the contrary, I understand that, if the most virtuous of Britons, let his place and authority be what they may, seize and hang up the greatest scoundrel in Her Majesty's dominions simply because he is an evil and troublesome person, an English court of justice will certainly find that virtuous person guilty of murder. Nor will the verdict be affected by any evidence that the defendant acted from the best of motives, and, on the whole, did the state a service. . . . I entertain so deeply-rooted an objection to this method of killing people—the act itself appears to me to be so frightful a precedent, that I desire to see it stigmatised by the highest authority as a crime. And I have joined the committee which proposes to indict Mr. Eyre, in the hope that I may hear a court of justice declare that the only defence which can be set up . . . is no defence, and that the killing of Mr. Gordon was the greatest offence known to the law—murder."[1]

[1] L. Huxley, *Life and Letters of Thomas Henry Huxley* (ed. 2, 1903), i. 404-5.

I should add that Eyre met with equally staunch defenders on the other side—Ruskin, Carlyle, and Tennyson among them : the case set half England by the ears. The Jamaica Committee's efforts failed. Eyre went free and died peacefully in Devonshire in 1901. What matters, however, is not the outcome of the case but the fact of the prosecutions : the clear warning they gave of the steady watchfulness of British public opinion, even on the domestic affairs of Jamaica.

The humanitarians' criticism has often been intemperate and ill-judged : in their turn they have come in for laughter and contempt. Hazlitt attacked Wilberforce as one who " preaches vital Christianity to untutored savages ; and tolerates its worst abuses in civilised states ".[1] Dickens scourged the promoters of the Niger Expedition of 1841 : " no amount of philanthropy has a right to waste such valuable life as was squandered here, in the teeth of all experience and feasible pretence of hope ".[2] A few years later he resumed the attack, not this time with his heavy guns but with the peppering fire of his ridicule. Mrs. Jellyby in *Bleak House* is an immortal busybody, high-minded and muddle-headed, her life given up to the most futile of good works. " She was a pretty, very diminutive, plump woman, of from forty to fifty, with handsome eyes, though they had a curious habit of seeming to look a long way off. As if . . . they could see nothing nearer than Africa ! ' You find me, my dears,' said Mrs. Jellyby, snuffing the two great office candles in tin candlesticks which made the room taste strongly of hot tallow (the fire had gone out, and there was nothing in the grate but ashes, a bundle of wood, and a poker), ' you find me, my

---

[1] *The Spirit of the Age* : in *Lectures on the English Poets,* etc. (" Everyman " ed.), 314.
[2] *Miscellaneous Papers* (1914), 123.

dears, as usual very busy; but that you will excuse. The African project at present employs my whole time. It involves me in correspondence with public bodies, and with private individuals anxious for the welfare of their species all over the country. I am happy to say it is advancing. We hope by this time next year to have from a hundred and fifty to two hundred healthy families cultivating coffee and educating the natives of Borrioboola-Gha, on the left bank of the Niger.' "[1]

The humanitarians certainly did not have it all their own way: nor did they deserve to. We all know Mrs. Jellybys still, and they have poked their noses into our colonial policy with particular vehemence and gusto. But for all their occasional absurdity, the humanitarians have surely exercised, on the whole, a most salutary influence on British imperialism. And not only by their watchful criticism and independent effort. Their ideas have permeated the administration in the Empire itself.

During the last hundred and fifty years, British colonial administrators have been among the best in the world. I will not say *the* best. It is impossible to make an exact comparison with, say, Belgian administrators since the great reform of 1908. Nor is there any need to attempt it: enough to say that the work of British civil servants stands extremely high. It was not always so. The early days of the East India Company's territorial dominion in Bengal were marked by abuses of every kind, put down with great difficulty by Warren Hastings and Cornwallis—under pressure, let us notice, from humanitarians in England. Even in the nineteenth century the quality of the administration in the more remote and unhealthy colonies was often poor. The pay was low, the incentives to enterprise few, for promotion was capricious: if he survived to a retiring

[1] *Bleak House* (Everyman ed.), 35-6.

age, the administrator got no pension, or a pitifully inadequate one. Not that that question often arose, for the mortality in such a colony as the Gambia or the Gold Coast was dreadful. You turn the pages of the correspondence in the Public Record Office today; you accustom yourself to the handwriting, you begin to discern the prejudices, of Governor Smith; the hand changes— Governor Smith has died of a fever and been replaced by Governor Brown; a few months more, or a year, and Brown is succeeded by Robinson. In such circumstances, continuity of policy was an idle dream, and planning ahead quite unthinkable. " Colonial administration " meant, for the administrators, very little more than a perpetually losing struggle to remain abreast of routine business, a despairing fight to keep life going at all. As a British official in one of these territories put it, with macabre humour, " the only reason that the officials of this colony remain alive is that there are no trees in it high enough to hang themselves upon ".[1]

It could hardly be expected that a life of this kind— I am afraid it was like life in Hobbes's state of nature, " solitary, poor, nasty, brutish, and short "—would attract any able men who could find better jobs elsewhere. Real progress in colonies of this kind became possible only with the gradual administrative reform that permitted an easy transfer of officials from one colony to another, so that they were not condemned to remain in one place all their lives ; and, even more vital, with the development of an effective treatment of disease and a sound Medical Service.

In India the same problems existed, but they were faced and overcome much earlier by a better organisation of the service, so that transfers were easier and more

[1] Quoted in H. L. Hall, *The Colonial Office* (1937), 116.

frequent, and by very much higher pay. English civil servants no longer went to India to make great fortunes—that was something that disappeared in the eighteenth century. But the pay was just high enough to enable the Government of India to compete on equal terms, year after year, for the ablest men in England, and to secure a high proportion of them. If you look carefully into the salaries that these men received, and set against them their expenditure—the big establishments they had to keep, the frequent and heavy expense of moving stations, the education of their children in England, many more things of the same kind—you will soon see that the net reward of their service was adequate, and no more.[1]

They expected and they secured, then, a decent wage. Many of them, no doubt, thought of that first: they did their jobs competently and retired in due course to Cheltenham or Bath or Bedford. But routineers like that are not typical of the Indian Civil Servants of the nineteenth century. Their true characteristics were ceaseless hard work and a cheerful, ungrudging service to the people for whom they were responsible. Take one instance, from an account of the early days of British rule in the Punjab—when that astonishing handful of men, led by the Lawrences, brought the whole country under a settled and just administration in spite of the bitter legacy of the conquest. Looking back to those days, one of the Lawrences' subordinates said, " I seem still to have a sort of feeling of ubiquity. A good stable was an essential equipment. If in the remotest corner of the District there occurred a cow-riot or an affray or a murder or a big burglary, the Deputy Commissioner or an Assistant had to be on the spot. If cholera broke out, every village affected had to be visited.

[1] Cf. Lord Beveridge, *India Called Them* (1947), 195-8 and table opposite p. 182.

No remission of revenue was ever granted without a personal inspection of the land and the crops. . . . It was an unwritten law that the Civil Officers should see things with their own eyes, do things with their own hands, and inquire into things for themselves. Thus they came to know the people, the people learned to know them, and a grip was got on the country which the Mutiny of 1857 did not loosen."[1]

That account is characteristic not only of the kind of work these men did but of the affectionate solicitude they felt for their people. They grumbled, all of them, at times, at the climate, at the remoteness of India, at the disappointing unreliability of Indians. But they loved the country none the less, and many of them left their hearts there. As one of them put it : " At times when I sit in the garden in the cool of the evening . . . I feel as if I never could go home. India has burnt itself into me."[2]

The man who wrote those words was not, indeed, at all a typical Indian Civil Servant. He was Henry Beveridge, father of Lord Beveridge, who spent more than thirty years of his life as magistrate and judge in Bengal. He had no sentimental illusions about the people he worked among. " The besetting sin of the Bengalis ", he wrote, " is that they will think and talk and talk and think for ever, but that they will not act. But then this is the very reason we are here, for if Bengalis could only act half as well as they talk there would be no need for us Westerns to rule over them. We must therefore take them as we find them and do our best for them."[3]

" *There would be no need for us Westerns to rule over them.*" In that sentence lies the difference between Beveridge and

---

[1] Sir Charles Aitchison, quoted in L. S. S. O'Malley, *The Indian Civil Service 1601-1930* (1931), 190-1.
[2] Lord Beveridge, *India Called Them*, 234.
[3] ibid., 96.

nearly all his contemporaries. For he always looked forward to a day in the future when the Indians would be able to rule themselves, and his view was that Britain's function in India was temporary : that it should be her objective to work as directly and quickly as possible for the extinction of her own power. Now these ideas were not new. They had been held, and held widely, in the 1820s and 1830s. Macaulay had stated them in the glowing, majestic peroration of his great speech on the Government of India Bill of 1833 : " It may be that the public mind of India may expand under our system till it has outgrown that system ; that by good government we may educate our subject's into a capacity for better government, that, having become instructed in European knowledge, they may, in some future age, demand European institutions. Whether such a day will ever come I know not. But never will I attempt to avert or to retard it. Whenever it comes, it will be the proudest day in English history. To have found a great people sunk in the lowest depths of slavery and superstition, to have so ruled them as to have made them desirous and capable of all the privileges of citizens, would indeed be a title to glory all our own. . . ."[1] How moving it was to turn back to those words when the Indian Independence Act was passing through Parliament in 1947!

By Henry Beveridge's time, by the sixties and seventies, sentiments of that sort had gone out of fashion. The Mutiny had a deadly effect in opening up a much wider chasm between Englishmen and Indians than had ever existed before. The efficiency, the honesty, the kindliness of the administration remained intact ; but its outlook became wholly paternal. Britain held a trust for the welfare of the people of India. She exercised it with care and prudence, and generally with justice. But it was not really

[1] Macaulay, *Speeches* (1854), 163.

looked on as a temporary trust, which would expire when the ward came of age : nine Indian Civil Servants in ten thought of it as permanent. Beveridge was a rare exception. And so it came about that, while a few Englishmen still contemplated self-government in India as a desirable and attainable goal, they were generally regarded as eccentric, even disloyal ; and the leadership of what became a protracted and bitter struggle passed wholly into Indian hands.

I have said little so far of self-government in the British Empire—by common consent the greatest contribution that Britain has made to the political practice of the world. I have left it to the end, partly because it is, I think, a more familiar theme than some of those I have been touching on, and partly because it is most fitting to consider it as the crown of Britain's imperial achievement.

English colonisation, from its very beginning in the New World, in the early years of the seventeenth century, contained unusual elements of self-government. Unusual, that is, when compared with the practice and theory of other European states. It was in 1619 that the first representative assembly met in Virginia, closely modelled, in constitution and procedure, on the Parliament of England. One after another the little English colonies in North America and the West Indies imitated Virginia's example as the century went on. But no other colonies. It is not for another two centuries that a permanent and regularly-constituted representative body appears in any other empire than Britain's. The powers of these assemblies were closely restricted in law, it is true ; but they were in practice very wide. It was largely because they were so wide that the people of the Thirteen Colonies in the late eighteenth century sought to make them wider, and so precipitated the American Revolution.

That Revolution taught Britain a most salutary lesson.
It was the fear of a repetition of it in Canada that led to
the wise concession of self-government. And from that
concession in Canada sprang the similar responsible
government in Australia, New Zealand, the Union of
South Africa. In our own time the process has been worked
out, on somewhat different lines, in India and Ceylon. And
we are seeing it on the way in the West Indies, in some
territories in Africa, and in South-East Asia.

Perhaps we may now return to the question I put
forward as my main text. Is there a specifically British
imperial tradition, and if so where are we to look for it?
I believe there is, and I have tried to indicate some of the
elements of which I think it is composed. Some of them,
not all : for I have not discussed a number of things that
are important—the emigration from Britain to her colonies,
to take only one example, which has been on a far greater
scale than that from other European countries to theirs.
But already it seems to me that something may be plainly
discerned. The British Empire is one founded on trade, and
at all times maintained by it ; a civilian empire, not a
military one as the German empire was, or as the French to
some extent is still. Public opinion, and especially humanitarian opinion, has constantly played upon British imperial
policy, helped to make and reform it. The idea of the trust,
held by the rulers on behalf of their subjects, has been deeply
implanted in the minds of British colonial administrators :
it has made them—if I may use the phrase—trust-worthy,
but it has also tended to make them cautious and conservative. That conservative principle has been leavened,
however, by one still stronger : the principle of self-
government, the recognition that however well alien
administrators are doing their job, every people likes to
rule itself all the same—preferring, if there must be a

choice, to rule itself badly rather than to be ruled well by others. Those principles are none of them peculiar to Britain. But the combination of them is unique, and it is that which makes up the British imperial tradition.

# APPENDIX I

A LIST of the buildings designed by John Johnson was printed by Nichols in his *History of Leicestershire*.[1] There is good reason to suppose that it was supplied by Johnson himself. It is minute, and clearly drawn up with greater care than Nichols could ever have given to it ; and he had, besides, a connexion with Nichols, which no doubt arose from their common interest in Leicestershire. Johnson's *Plans* of the Chelmsford Shire Hall were published by Nichols, and he presented one of the plates to Nichols' *History* (vol. i, no. xxxv). I give the list here, arranged alphabetically under counties, with a few additions (shown in italics) and some comments. It does not include his bridges, which are discussed in the text above.

## DEVON

KILLERTON HOUSE : parish of Broad Clyst. "It was built as a temporary residence by Sir Thomas Acland, who died in 1788, and has been enlarged and improved by his grandson, the present baronet."[2]

## DORSET

SADBOROUGH HOUSE : parish of Thorncombe (transferred from Devon in 1842), for William Bragg.[3]

[1] Vol. i, p. 528.
[2] D. and S. Lysons, *Magna Britannia : Devonshire* (1822), 115.
[3] J. Hutchins, *History and Antiquities of the County of Dorset* (ed. 3, 1861-1870), iv. 529.

## ESSEX

BARKING : *House of Correction.*

BRADWELL-JUXTA-MARE : an extension of the old rectory, made to the orders of the Rev. Henry Bate-Dudley (1745-1824), who bought the advowson of the living in 1781 and presented himself to it in 1797.[1]

BROOMFIELD : house for John Judd, apparently built on an estate in this parish called Gutters.[2]

CHELMSFORD : Shire Hall, *House of Correction, Parish Church* (rebuilding). See pp. 131, 135-6.

HATFIELD PEVEREL : house for Colonel Tyrell.

LANGFORD GROVE : parish of Langford, $2\frac{1}{2}$ miles north of Maldon. Built for N. Westcombe and now un-occupied.

TERLING PLACE : parish of Terling. Built for John Strutt, who purchased the estate from Sir Matthew Featherstone-haugh in 1761.[3] The centre portion is said to have been erected by John Strutt soon after he bought the property : the wings were added by his son.[4]

STROUD GREEN HOUSE : parish of Rochford. Now called " The Lawn ". Johnson here built additional rooms on to an earlier house, under the direction of the owner, Major G. D. Carr, of the Essex Militia.[5]

TORRILE'S HALL : parish of East Thurrock, for John Crabb.

WILLINGALE DOE : house for the Rev. John Bramston-Stane.

[1] *Essex Review*, vi. 208 ; and for Bate-Dudley's fascinating career see the *Dictionary of National Biography*.

[2] T. Wright, *History and Topography of the County of Essex* (1836), i. 188.

[3] P. Morant, *History of Essex* (1768), ii. 126.

[4] J. A. Rush, *Seats in Essex* [1897], 173.

[5] P. Benton, *History of Rochford Hundred* [1873], 848-9.

## GLAMORGAN

CLASSMOUNT : house near Morriston, for John Morris.[1]
GNOLL CASTLE, NEAR NEATH : for Sir Herbert Mackworth.[2]


## LEICESTERSHIRE

*Knighton Hall, Leicester*: part of the front of the house, added
  on to an existing building. (The work is attributed to
  Johnson by Professor A. E. Richardson, R.A.)
LEICESTER : Consanguinitarium, County Rooms, *Theatre*
  (1800-1836), Town Gaol. These buildings are discussed
  on pp. 137-42.
WHATTON HALL : parish of Long Whatton, for Edward
  Dawson.[3]


## LONDON AND MIDDLESEX

HOUSES IN CAVENDISH STREET, Portland Place, for the
  Earl of Hardwicke and William Udney.
HOUSES IN HARLEY STREET for the Bishop of Ossory and
  John Pybus.
HOUSE IN PALL MALL for Sir Hugh Palliser.
HOUSES IN PORTMAN SQUARE for the Hon. Charles Greville
  and Lord Middleton.
HOUSE IN ST. JAMES'S SQUARE for the Earl of Galloway.
HOUSE AT MILL HILL, Middlesex, for Sir John Anderson
  (subsequently occupied by Sir Stamford Raffles).

[1] *Beauties of South Wales* (1815), 720.
[2] ibid., 711 ; C. B. Andrews (ed.), *The Torrington Diaries* (1934-1938), i. 298.
[3] See the view in Nichols, iii. 1105.

## NORTHAMPTONSHIRE

East Carlton Hall : for Sir John Palmer.

Kingsthorpe Hall : for James Fremeaux.[1]   Now the property of the Borough of Northampton.

Pitsford Hall : for Colonel Money.


## SUFFOLK

Benhall Lodge : for Sir William Rush of Wimbledon, Surrey, who succeeded his uncle, Samuel Rush, in 1781. The house is said to have cost him £15,000. It was sold to Admiral Sir Hyde Parker (1739-1807). The manor was bought in 1810 by Edward Hollond, who pulled Johnson's house down and replaced it by another.[2]

Newmarket : Noblemen's and Gentlemen's Club Rooms.

Woolverstone Hall : for William Berners. This fine house now belongs to the L.C.C. and is used as a boarding school. It retains much of its original decoration : the ceilings are particularly notable.


## SURREY

Wimbledon Church : rebuilt by Johnson in 1787.[3]


## SUSSEX

Seat of Charles Beauclerk. I have not been able to identify this house.

[1] V. C. H. *Northants.*, iv. 83.
[2] W. A. Copinger, *The Manors of Suffolk* (1905-1911), v. 104.
[3] See the view of the church, dated 1809, reproduced in V. C. H. *Surrey*, vi. 524. It was again rebuilt in 1833-1834 : E. W. Brayley, *Topographical History of Surrey* (n.d.), iii. 504.

In HIS *History of the Great Western Railway* (vol. ii, p. 489) Mr. MacDermot prints a table showing the shortest times between Paddington and some of the principal stations on the railway in 1888, 1900, and 1912. He chose the year 1888 as the first in which the new improvements in the train service appeared (see p. 173); 1900 as the last in which all the old devious main lines were in use; 1912 as that which saw all the new short cuts brought into effective operation. I reproduce his table here, extended so as to include two more years: 1939, the last before the Second World War; and 1951, giving the times in the summer service.

An examination of the figures in this table gives one a good deal to think about. The general tendency is clear enough: a steady, sometimes a spectacular, improvement between 1888 and 1912; a much smaller one by 1939; a falling off in 1951. But there are some exceptions, and one of them is important. The service to Chester and Birkenhead shows very little real change. It is true that by 1912 the time to Chester was 35 minutes less than in 1888, and that to Birkenhead had come down by 18 minutes. But 18¾ miles had been taken off the journey through the opening of the new Birmingham main line via Bicester in 1910. In 1951 the quickest train from Paddington actually takes 10 minutes longer to Chester, and 27 minutes longer to Birkenhead, *over this substantially shorter route*, than the quickest train of 1888: or to put it another way, the average speed (inclusive of stops) has come down from 44.7 m.p.h. in 1888 to 37.7 m.p.h. in 1951. It is not a sufficient answer to point out that this journey can be made more quickly by the Western Region line from Euston, for (1) by nearly all the best trains it is necessary to change at Crewe, and for Birkenhead at Chester as well; and (2) Chester and Birkenhead are only two stations on a long main line: the service to other towns on it, e.g. Oswestry and Wrexham, has become similarly slower, and they have no alternative route.

On the whole, the 1951 figures in this table are a depressing set compared with those of 1912, let alone those of 1939: 22 minutes longer to Worcester, 23 to Tenby and Plymouth, 29 to Shrewsbury. But let us be scrupulously fair to the Railway Executive (Western Region). They have difficulties to contend with in 1951— in supplies, in arrears of maintenance, and in many other ways—that never faced the Great Western in 1912. And a table such as this shows only one thing: the time taken by the fastest trains. That is no more than one factor in forming a judgment on the total service that is provided. It is plainly better to have six trains in the day at 40 m.p.h. than one at 50 and three at 30: yet in a table of this kind the second service would appear to be better than the first. A full comparison, taking all the relevant considerations into account, would be a much more elaborate affair: perhaps it would be impossible to make.

The Table is printed on pp. 248-9.

# SHORTEST TIMES BETWEEN PADDINGTON AND SOME PRINCIPAL STATIONS

## 1888, 1900, 1912, 1939, AND 1951

| Station | 1888 Dist. miles | 1888 Time h. m. | 1900 Dist. miles | 1900 Time h. m. | 1912 Dist. miles | 1912 Time h. m. | 1939 Dist. miles | 1939 Time h. m. | 1951 Dist. miles | 1951 Time h. m. |
|---|---|---|---|---|---|---|---|---|---|---|
| READING | 36 | 46 | | 44 | | 42 | | 40 | | 41 |
| BATH | 107 | 2 15[1] | | 1 58 | | 1 48 | | 1 42 | | 1 53 |
| BRISTOL | 118¼ | 2 36[1] | | 2 15 | | 2 0 | | 1 45 | | 2 10 |
| TAUNTON | 163¼ | 3 32[1] | | 3 25 | 143 | 2 30 | | 2 20 | | 2 28 |
| ILFRACOMBE | 224½ | 7 2 | | 6 36 | 203¾ | 5 18 | | 5 10 | | 5 38 |
| EXETER | 194 | 4 14[1] | 193¾ | 3 43 | 173¾ | 3 0 | | 2 50 | | 3 3 |
| TORQUAY | 220 | 5 12[1] | 219¾ | 4 50 | 199¾ | 3 53 | | 3 30 | | 3 45 |
| PLYMOUTH[2] | 246 | 5 50[1] | 245¾ | 5 7 | 225¾ | 4 7 | | 4 5 | | 4 30 |
| NEWQUAY | 302½ | 8 36[1] | 301 | 7 25 | 281 | 6 35 | | 6 10 | | 6 35[3] |
| PENZANCE | 326½ | 8 55[1] | 325 | 8 32 | 305¼ | 6 35 | | 6 30 | | 6 55 |
| WEYMOUTH | 168¾ | 4 45[1] | | 4 15 | 154½ | 3 10 | | 3 7 | | 3 27 |
| GLOUCESTER | 114 | 2 52 | | 2 39 | | 2 30 | | 2 2 | | 2 22 |
| CHELTENHAM | 121½[4] | 3 15 | 109[5] | 2 45 | | 2 37 | 121½[4] | 2 20 | | 2 45 |
| NEWPORT | 143½ | 3 57 | | 2 57 | 133½ | 2 30 | | 2 21 | | 2 34[6] |
| CARDIFF | 155¼ | 4 17 | | 3 17 | 145¼ | 2 50 | | 2 41 | | 2 42 |
| SWANSEA | 201 | 5 55 | | 4 45 | 191 | 4 0 | | 3 57 | | 4 1 |
| TENBY | 259½ | 7 50 | | 7 35 | 249½ | 5 50 | | 6 3 | | 6 13[7] |

[1] First and second class only. The best third-class times were : Bath, 2 h. 23 m. ; Bristol, 2 h. 44 m. ; Taunton, 3 h. 46 m. ; Exeter, 4 h. 37 m. ; Torquay, 5 h. 50 m. ; Plymouth (Millbay), 6 h. 30 m. ; Newquay, 10 h. 40 m. ; Penzance, 10 h. 35 m. ; Weymouth, 5 h. 0 m.

[2] North Road station.

[3] Fridays and Saturdays only : 6 h. 40 m. Mondays-Thursdays.

[4] Via Swindon and Gloucester.

[5] Via Oxford and Kingham.

[6] Saturdays only : 2 h. 35 m. Mondays-Fridays.

[7] Saturdays only : 6 h. 32 m. Mondays-Fridays.

## SHORTEST TIMES BETWEEN PADDINGTON AND SOME PRINCIPAL STATIONS (Cont'd)
### 1888, 1900, 1912, 1939, AND 1951

| Station | 1888 | | 1900 | | 1912 | | 1939 | | 1951 | |
|---|---|---|---|---|---|---|---|---|---|---|
| | Dist. | Time | Dist. | Time | Dist. | Time | Dist. | Time | Dist. | Time |
| | miles | h. m. | miles | h. m. | miles | h. m. | miles | h. m. | miles | h. m. |
| OXFORD | 63½ | 1 18 | | 1 17 | | 1 10 | | 1 0 | | 1 12 |
| WORCESTER | 120½ | 3 0 | | 2 15 | | 2 9 | | 2 10 | | 2 31 |
| HEREFORD | 144$\frac{11}{4}$ | 4 13 | 149$\frac{32}{4}$ | 3 20 | | 3 15 | | 3 4 | | 3 30 |
| LEAMINGTON | 106 | 2 13 | | 1 57 | 87¼ | 1 31 | | 1 30 | | 1 43 |
| BIRMINGHAM | 129¼ | 2 42 | | 2 25 | 110½ | 2 0 | | 2 0 | | 2 10 |
| WOLVER-HAMPTON | 141¾ | 3 4 | | 2 50 | 123 | 2 24 | | 2 25 | | 2 35 |
| SHREWSBURY | 171½ | 3 51 | | 3 35 | 152¾ | 2 59 | | 3 9 | | 3 28[3] |
| BARMOUTH | 251½ | 7 35 | | 6 25 | 232¾ | 6 2 | | 6 7 | | 6 26[4] |
| CHESTER | 213¾ | 4 50 | | 4 50 | 195 | 4 15 | | 4 19 | | 5 0 |
| BIRKENHEAD | 229¼ | 5 8 | | 5 17 | 210½ | 4 50 | | 4 47 | | 5 35 |

N.B.—Where no distance is shown, it may be taken to be the same as in the preceding entry.

[1] Via Swindon and Gloucester.
[2] Via Oxford and Worcester.
[3] Saturdays only: 3 h. 41 m. Mondays-Fridays.
[4] Saturdays only: 6 h. 35 m. Mondays-Fridays.

# INDEX